YEADON'S REGISTER

of

L N E R

LOCOMOTIVES

Volume Twenty

**Class Q1, Q2, Q3 & Q4,
& The Q1 Tank**

YEADON'S REGISTER OF L.N.E.R. LOCOMOTIVES - VOLUME 20

EDITOR'S NOTE & ACKNOWLEDGEMENTS

So far, within the twenty volumes of *Yeadon's Register* already published, some 3200-odd LNER locomotives contained within sixty-odd classes have been covered. Basically that figure represents approximately half of the total number of locomotives handed over by the LNER to British Railways at Nationalisation. So, we could say that we are half way through the series. However, that is not quite the case as most of you will realise because when the LNER came into being on 1st January 1923 that company inherited just over 7,400 locomotives - if one includes the Departmental, electric, petrol and assorted odds and ends. Moreover, during each year between 1923 and 1947, and even beyond to the early 1950's, some 2,300-odd new locomotives to LNER designs were added to stock. The balance leaves about 3,200-odd locomotives which were withdrawn during the lifetime of the LNER. In essence we are dealing with nine and a half thousand engines which belonged at one time or another to the LNER. Therefore, in reality, the Register has only covered just over a third of the total LNER locomotive fleet! Does this mean another forty or so Registers still to come? Not quite because many of those 'withdrawn' engines went for scrap well before World War Two, many during the 1920's and most of those had 'short' histories, so some of the future volumes will contain more locomotive histories than has otherwise been the case to date. Volume 21, for instance, will cover 211 engines whilst subsequent volumes will contain sometimes less engines and sometimes more; the latter will be the norm. Whatever, we will strive to complete the series with the same accuracy and attention to detail as WBY intended. For those who may be wondering how many volumes it will eventually require to complete the series, the number will probably be in the high thirties.

At which point you may appreciate the work that Eric Fry puts in checking the endless sheets of type, not just the numbers making up the tables but also the captions and potted history of the Introduction - all have to be correct. Where facts are less than clear they are left out rather than included for the sake of it. But, we are not saying that we are 100% correct in every aspect of this series so if any reader spots a mistake please feel free to write to the publisher pointing out our solecism.

Brian Dyson and the staff at the University of Hull Archive Department are forever ready to receive requests from the publishers and nothing, it seems, is too much trouble. Thanks.

Thanks also to Mike Lake who has come out of retirement to lend a hand; also Mick for pointing the way - we'll get you next time.

Annie, Jean and Simon - always in the background but never forgotten - thankyou.

And you, the reader, thanks also. Your enthusiasm is not faltering.

The next Register, Volume 21, will feature the tank engines of classes A5 to A8, H1, H2, L1 (L3), L2, M1 and M2.

The Yeadon Collection is available for inspection and anyone who wishes to inspect it should contact:-
The Archivist
Brynmor Jones Library
University of Hull
Hull
HU6 7RX
Tel: 01482-465265
A catalogue of the Yeadon collection is available.

First published in the United Kingdom by
BOOKLAW/RAILBUS 2001 in association with CHALLENGER
382 Carlton Hill, Nottingham NG41JA.
www.booklawpublications.co.uk
www.booklawpublications.co.com

Printed and bound by The Amadeus Press, Cleckheaton.

INTRODUCTION

Classes Q1, Q2 and Q3.

The movement of coal was the reason behind the invention of the railway and during the 19th century the companies associated with such traffic were forever moving greater and greater tonnages. The Great Northern Railway was one of the prime movers of coal to London and by the turn of the century this traffic was so great that the company had to improve the main line to allow the movement and refuge of 60-wagon trains. By 1901 this had been carried out and to coincide with the improvements, H.A.Ivatt, the CME of the GNR brought out a locomotive, in February of that year, capable of moving these great loads.

No.401 was the first of fifty-five such 0-8-0 tender engines with 4ft 8in. diameter boilers which, from 1903, were interchangeable with the Atlantic tender engines of the 'Klondyke' class. In a two and a half year period from April 1902 another thirty-nine 0-8-0's were constructed at Doncaster and these numbers were further swelled in the period between 1906 and 1909 by another fifteen examples. Classified K1 by the GNR, the class was to be eventually split into three separate classes by reason of being either fitted with slide or piston valves or boiler size.

The last five, Nos.451 to 455, came out new with superheaters and piston valves and were to form the basis for improvements carried out later on the earlier engines of the class. The first engine of the class to be superheated was No.417 which had a Schmidt superheater fitted in 1908, piston valves and new 20in. diameter cylinders were put in at the same time. The superheating necessitated a 9in. extension to the front end of the frames and the addition of piston vales pitched the boiler 2in. higher thereby cutting down the chimney and dome cover heights from rail level. During LNER days some of the Q2's had J6 class chimneys fitted to reduce their overall height.

It must be mentioned that during the period of building these engines Doncaster did not assign works numbers in the same numerical sequence as the running numbers, consequently these works numbers do not follow consequently. In an earlier learned history on GNR locomotives, the works numbers of Nos.3422 and 3425 are transposed, but the official records kept by Doncaster gave them as 1008 and 1009 respectively.

The LNER split the GN K1's into two classes, Q1 and Q2, those with slide valves and either saturated or superheated boilers were Q1 class and those with piston valves and superheater became Q2 class. Besides those five which came out new with superheaters, the GN fitted a further forty-two engines with superheaters, the remaining eight never got a superheated boiler. One engine, No.420, which had been superheated and fitted with piston valves in 1911 was rebuilt by Gresley in 1914 with a larger (5ft 6in.) boiler of the type currently being fitted to his 2-6-0 engines. To go with the new boiler a new cab was necessary but the engine chassis was virtually unaltered. A further ten 0-8-0's were to be rebuilt to this standard but the order was cancelled in favour of more of the then new 2-6-0's (LNER K2). However, this solitary example became Class Q3 (GN Class K2) in LNER days and was the last of the GN 0-8-0 tender engines to remain in service. At Grouping there were forty Q1's, fourteen Q2's and a solitary Q3.

Between 1925 and 1929 nineteen Q1 engines with Schmidt superheater (Nos.3403, 3405, 3406, 3407, 3410, 3415, 3416, 3417, 3421, 3427, 3432, 3440, 3442, 3444, 3451, 3452, 3453, 3454 and 3455) were altered to Robinson type. No.402 had been changed to Robinson type by Gresley in 1912 whilst No.445 got the Doncaster 'straight-tube' version of superheater in 1913 and which it retained to withdrawal. Another Gresley type superheater, the 'twin tube', was fitted to three engines: No.450 in 1915; No.408 in 1916 and No.447 in 1917. Nos.3435 and 3443 were scrapped before they could be changed from Schmidt to Robinson type. Of the 'twin tube' engines, No.3447 got a Robinson type in April 1925 and No.3450 got the same in April 1930 whilst the other with this type, No.3408, retained it to withdrawal.

The allocation of these engines when first introduced was between New England, Colwick and Doncaster with the former shed having no less than twenty-six allocated, Colwick had eleven and Doncaster just three. Once all the class had been built some 60% of them were at New England whilst the rest were at Colwick. In 1917 ten of New England's engines were lent to Hull Dairycoates in the North Eastern to replaced NER 0-8-0's which had gone to France. It is believed that two GNR K1's also went to France at the same time but this is still to be confirmed.

Just before Grouping the allocation of the class saw them at three sheds with New England still having the lion's share with forty-two, Colwick was now down to seven and Ardsley had gained six. With the introduction of the Gresley 2-8-0's onto the coal trains to London, the New England allocation dwindled and the 0-8-0's gradually took up residence in the Nottingham and West Riding Districts. At Ardsley they were less than welcome and were eventually displaced though not entirely, by O4 and later Q4 engines.

Up to 1925 none of the Q1's or Q2's had been allocated to London District but King's Cross and Hornsey sheds had three of them for pick-up work. The one at King's Cross, No.3447, went to Hitchin in 1928 as did one of the Hornsey pair, No.3434. The other Hornsey engine, No.3435, was withdrawn from that shed in 1929. Most ended their days on coal trains though not on the main line hauls but on colliery trips.

Doncaster took care of the maintenance of these engines but in 1925 seven of the class were sent to Darlington for general overhauls.

The first engine of the class, No.401, was turned out from Doncaster in black livery with single red lining and brass rims on the splashers. All the others came out in the GN lined green, without brass rims. In 1906 No.401 changed to green livery but kept the polished brass splasher rims. In December 1912 a plain grey livery was adopted and all the 0-8-0's were subsequently changed to this livery as they went through Doncaster shops. From 1923 black with red lining became the standard and after 1928 just plain black was worn.

The 'N' suffix was placed behind the number on some engines from August 1923 until 3000 was added to the GN number from February 1924. Those seven shopped at Darlington in 1925 had the addition of Class K1 painted on their buffer beams.

Withdrawals started in April 1926 when No.3428 was scrapped. By 1931 all the saturated engines had gone as well as a good many of the superheated examples. In 1935 classes

One engine No.401 was built by the Great Northern Railway at Doncaster in February 1901 to haul sixty loaded coal wagon trains from Peterborough to London.

In December 1908 No.417 was fitted with a superheater of the Schmidt type along with piston instead of slide valves. It was also fitted with new cylinders in which cast steel piston heads and tail rods were provided. These needed a 9in. extension to the frames.

Q1 and Q2 were rendered extinct but the solitary Q3, No.3420 lasted until February 1937.

Class Q4

Designated Great Central Class 8A, this the first of the GC eight-coupled types comprised a total of 89 engines. They were designed by J.G.Robinson and built between 1902 and 1911 with Neilson & Co. supplying the first three, Nos.1052-54. These were followed by another thirty-three during 1903-4, five in 1905 and another thirteen in 1907, all built by Kitson & Co. In 1909 Gorton built fifteen of the class and during 1910-11 turned out another twenty before the appearance of the larger 2-8-0 of GC Class 8K saw the end of Class 8A production.

The Q4 had similarities to the GC 4-6-0's of Class 8 (LNER B5), though not in appearance. They used a similar boiler of 4ft 9in. diameter and cylinders of 19in. diameter. The firebox of the Q4 was deeper because of the smaller driving wheels. However, the 0-8-0 had a large overhang at either end and looked somewhat ungainly though otherwise it was a good engine in all respects.

The Robinson 21-element superheater was the usual for this class and all but eight were superheated from 1914 onwards with the LNER carrying on the job after 1923. The eight saturated engines could be distinguished from the majority by the fact that their chimneys were centrally positioned on the smokebox, the others had their chimneys moved further forward to allow room for the header in the smokebox. During their lifetimes many of the superheated engines later got saturated boilers before reverting back, in most cases, to the superheated type.

Six of the class got the 21in. diameter cylinders which were standard on the 8K (LNER O4) class. Starting with No.1134 in 1916, the other five (5136, 5137, 5153, 5160 and 6076) did not receive theirs until LNER days and then it was 1928 before the first, No.5136, was fitted but another three years elapsed before any more were done. When No.5153 received its 21in. cylinders in May 1933, no more were done as the class was being earmarked for withdrawal, starting the following year.

The first forty-one engines were coupled to 3250 gallon tenders but the later built engines from 1907 onwards received the 4000 gallons type. All the engines built prior to 1907 received 4000 gallon tenders during the early years of the LNER although No.5146 got one at some time before Grouping. By 1930 all had the larger tender, however, at a later date No.5057 reverted to a 3250 gallon tender until 1943. Nearly all of the class had water pick-up apparatus but from 1939 authority was given to have this equipment removed. Wartime saw the order withdrawn but in 1946 removal began in earnest. It is thought that a couple of the Q4's actually retained the water pick-up gear to withdrawal during the BR period.

Haulage of heavy goods, especially coal trains, was their job on the GCR and the allocations reflect this fact. Most could be found at sheds situated within the coalfields of South Yorkshire and Nottinghamshire with a few resident on the west side of the Pennines at Gorton. Mexborough shed had forty-one of the class at Grouping.

Fifteen engines were sent on loan to Railway Operating Division in France in 1917 to help the war effort on the Western Front. All returned intact to the GC in 1919, though in need of overhaul.

When large numbers of the Robinson designed 2-8-0's (LNER O4) became available from the Ministry of Munitions shortly after Grouping many of the Q4's were displaced from the former GC line sheds and ended their days in the West Riding at sheds such as Bradford and Ardsley. At the latter depot they became favourites of the enginemen who much preferred them to the GN designs. With a touch of irony, the Q4's actually replaced the recently arrived O4's at Ardsley where the turntable was not large enough to accommodate the 2-8-0's. By the end of 1939 Ardsley had fourteen of the surviving fifty Q4's on its books. The next highest number was Langwith Junction with ten allocated, then Mexborough with eight, Barnsley with six, Immingham with four and two each at Bradford, Frodingham, Retford and Staveley. By 1941 the two at Bradford had joined the fourteen at Ardsley. Typically, wartime saw the Q4's working into areas which were not usually associated with the class and both Newcastle and Edinburgh had visits from one or two of the class. In the latter period of WWII some of those based at East Midlands sheds were occasionally seen in the London area having worked down the ECML. Whilst New England got six of them in 1943 it is not known if any worked south to the Capital. From August 1944 the half dozen at New England began working over the M&GN lines to Melton Constable and even further east, the only 0-8-0's ever to have regularly done so. For these working they were fitted with tablet catchers. By October 1945 these six returned to the GC Section. In 1946 Grantham shed acquired six which were joined later by three more. Grantham fitted tablet catchers to the tender so that the Q4's could work the iron ore trains over the High Dyke branch. In 1950 the Q4's still at Grantham, then numbering six, left and went to Ardsley which became the last stronghold of the class.

During Edward Thompson's tenure as CME the whole class were chosen to become 0-8-0 tank shunting engines classified Q1 but only thirteen Q4's were converted during the years 1942 to 1945 before the scheme was halted.

The addition of a 'C' suffix in 1923-4 involved some of the class. However, it must be stressed that it is by no means certain that any of the following engines actually carried the suffix. Those engines surmised to have done so were: 58c 22/9; 138c 22/12; 143c 15/12; 148c 20/10; 213c 29/12; 957c 15/12; 965c 20/10; 1073c 22/12; 1075c 10/11; 1077c 20/10; 1136c 17/11; 1142c 1/12; 1182c 22/12, all 1923. No.962c apparently got the suffix in January 1924.

5000 was added to the numbers of the Q4's in the 1924 renumbering and the known dates are given in the tables but again a few unknowns have crept in regarding Nos.5138, 5213, 5965 and 6073; these particular engines are quoted as being renumbered as late as 1927 but it is probable that they were in fact renumbered earlier.

Regarding the 1946 numbering, this was straightforward as regards the official list drawn up in 1943 but it will be noted that a number of the converted engines which became Q1 tanks were actually allocated numbers in the Q4 series before their conversion date hence the gaps (besides one withdrawal) in the Q4 list once renumbering had started in January 1946. Of the original forty-four numbers allocated to the Q4's, Nos.3200 to 3243, ten were never used.

LNER livery was black with single red lining up to 1928 but few of the class got this and remained in the black carried over from GC days. The painting economies of 1928 did not affect the Q4's and they wore the black paint to withdrawal. NE replaced LNER during wartime but even this was better

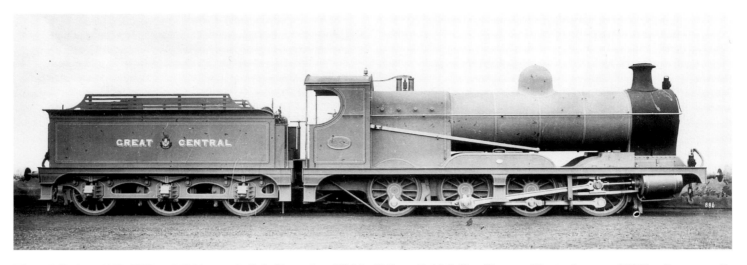

Three Q4's, Nos.1052, 1053 and 1054, were built in November 1902 by Neilson, Reid & Co., Glasgow. The tender was of 3250 gallons capacity with pick-up apparatus. Boiler and cylinders were similar to those on engines which became Class B5 being built concurrently by this firm. Only these three had taper shank buffers.

One engine No.5058, ex Doncaster 25th June 1942 was converted from Q4 Class to provide a heavy shunter and release a tender for use elsewhere.

than the pre-Group period when they did not even wear the GC company crest.

Withdrawals started in 1934 and by the outbreak of war in September 1939 nearly half the class had been condemned. However, their usefulness during the war years ensured that many of the 1939 survivors became British Railways property, albeit for only a few years of Nationalisation but nevertheless some survived until 1951 when the design was nearly fifty years old. Indeed one of the initial trio of engines built by Neilson & Co. in 1902 (GCR No.1054) was not withdrawn until January 1951 as No.63201. The class became extinct when No.63243 was withdrawn from Ardsley shed in October in that same year.

Class Q1 Tank

In November 1941 a new 0-8-0 tank engine design for heavy shunting duties was drawn up. Designated Class Q1, the engines would be rebuilds of the Class Q4 0-8-0's. Initially all the remaining Q4's were to be rebuilt to Q1 but the first two orders, issued in early 1942, encompassed just twenty-five engines. In the event only thirteen engines were converted between 1942 and 1945, all at Doncaster.

The conversions released the tenders for use elsewhere, a couple became water carriers at Woodford Halse whilst the rest went back to Gorton as spares.

Three engines, Nos.5058, 5961 and 6139, were converted in 1942, followed by No.5048 early in 1943. The design was then modified so as to increase the water capacity. The frames were lengthened by 6in. at the rear end which enabled a larger sphere of operations. Nos.5070 and 6077, were thus rebuilt at the end of 1943. 1944 saw four converted, Nos.5044, 5068, 5087 and 5959, whilst the last three, Nos.5138, 5147 and 6179, emerged from Doncaster in 1945. In 1946 the first four conversions were classified Part 1, the nine rebuilt later becoming Part 2.

No less than thirty-one Diagram 17A boilers were available for use on this class. Twenty-six new boilers had been built by Gorton during the 1942-45 period and five of the original Diagram 17 boilers taken off the converted Q4's were altered by Doncaster to Dia.17A. These numbers reflect the initial orders for twenty-five engines, with six spare boilers. Eventually, after the conversions ceased the surplus boilers were either cut up or used as stationery boilers. The eventual boiler stock for the class was fifteen by 1951, all of the saturated type.

All except Nos.5147 and 6139, which came out with Group Standard type, kept GC type front buffers at the conversion. No.69925 (5058) was later to have GS buffers fitted to the front beam at a Cowlairs overhaul in 1951, the only one so altered. The rear buffers on all the Q1 tanks were GS by necessity of being new.

Initially all the class were allocated at Southern Area sheds but not at the same time. Frodingham, Langwith Junction and Mexborough being the main associations whilst Ardsley, Barnsley and Retford had some of them for short periods. No.5058 was sent to Eastfield in August 1943 along with No.6139 after the latter engine had spent three weeks on loan to the Scottish depot in April of that year. These two engines stayed at the Glasgow shed until withdrawal. Two went to North Eastern Area in September 1944, No.5044 to Selby and No.5087 to Hull Dairycoates. At the end of the year they both went to Gateshead for just over four years before they returned south to Selby where they stayed until withdrawal, hump

shunting at Gascoigne Wood yard. No.5961 spent much of its early years on the Great Eastern Section working the yards at both March and Cambridge. It went to Frodingham in April 1951 and stayed there until withdrawal. Another Q1, No.69930, spent five months at Stratford during 1950, shunting at Temple Mills yard. The others all settled down to work, eventually, from Frodingham, Immingham and Langwith Junction sheds but prior to that six of them were at Mexborough working coal trains from Wath yard to Rotherwood yard. They were not liked at Mexborough where the footplate crews detested the cramped cabs and found them unsuitable for the Rotherwood trips because of the inadequate water capacity of the tanks. Braking was something of a problem too whenever steep gradients were encountered. Doncaster received the Mexborough engines in August 1946 when they stayed just a month before being passed on to Frodingham where the heavy steel and minerals traffic required more than just an 0-6-0 tank engine. No.69926 joined the six at Frodingham, moving from March shed in April 1951 and eventually Frodingham housed all the Eastern Region based engines when the two at Langwith Junction moved to there in June 1958.

Maintenance was carried out at three different works, Cowlairs for the two Scottish engines, Darlington for the two North East based engines and Gorton for the Southern Area engines. From 1952 those engines based in the North Eastern Region were also shopped at Gorton.

Initially the engines came out with a cast totem style plate fixed on the rear bunker side and bearing the letters LNER with a blue background but after Nationalisation these were removed from the England based engines whilst the Scottish duo kept them to withdrawal.

Livery throughout was black unlined and the addition of 60000 to their numbers was effected during 1948 and 1949 except for the Eastfield based 9925 which was not brought into line until April 1951.

Withdrawals started in 1954 when 69925 was, ironically, condemned at Cowlairs because a replacement boiler could not be found. No more were withdrawn until 1956 when two, 69927 and 69937 succumbed. 1958 saw five more withdrawn whilst the last five were condemned in 1959, the class becoming extinct on 15th September when 69936 was withdrawn from Frodingham shed and sent to Darlington for scrapping.

Twenty further engines to the same specifications as No.401, Nos.402 to 421, were built at Doncaster between March 1902 and January 1903. Their designer H.A.Ivatt is seen here showing No.405 to Archibald Sturrock, who was GNR Locomotive Engineer from 1850 to 1866, when he retired. Note safety chains and hooks were still being fitted.

Superheating began in December 1908, No.406 being fitted in July 1912 with a Schmidt type. At the same time it was also changed from flat to piston valves, and a mechanical lubricator was put on. This engine was the first to have anti-vacuum valves, two being mounted behind the chimney and connected to the saturated side of the header. Use of piston valves led to the LNER classifying them separately as Q2.

Nineteen more engines, Nos.422 to 440 were built at Doncaster from June 1903 to September 1904 and were similar to the previous engines. From October 1912 to January 1920 all except Nos.428, 431, 433, 434, 437 and 439 were superheated but, none of this batch were rebuilt with piston valves. Only Nos.422, 425, 427, 432, 435 and 440 first got the twin pepper pot type anti-vacuum valves.

CLASSES Q 1, Q 2 & Q 3

3401

Doncaster 923.

To traffic 2/1901.

REPAIRS:
Don. ?/?—12/05.**G.**
Don. ?/?—13/1/16.**G.**
Superheater put in.
Don. 5/12/23—19/4/24.**G.**
Don. 7/2—15/12/27.**G.**

BOILERS:
401.
1572 ?/12/05.
8048 *(new)* 15/12/27.

SHED:
Colwick.

RENUMBERED:
3401 19/4/24.

CONDEMNED: 20/6/29.
Cut up at Doncaster.

3402

Doncaster 964.

To traffic 3/1902.

REPAIRS:
Don. ?/?—22/4/12.**G.**
Rebuilt to Q2.
Don. 30/8—3/12/21.**G.**
Don. 13/6—25/10/24.**G.**

BOILERS:
1392.
7133 *(superheated)* 22/4/12.

SHED:
Colwick.

RENUMBERED:
3402 25/10/24.

CONDEMNED: 13/9/27.
Cut up at Doncaster.

3403

Doncaster 968.

To traffic 4/1902.

REPAIRS:
Don. ?/?—1/11.**G.**

Don. ?/?—29/5/13.**G.**
Don. 12/2—2/6/23.**G.**
Don. 9/3—19/6/26.**G.**

BOILERS:
1393.
1551 ?/1/11.
7194 *(superheated)* 29/5/13.
7833 19/6/26.

SHEDS:
Doncaster.
Ardsley ?/?

RENUMBERED:
3403 19/6/26.

CONDEMNED: 10/6/29.
Cut up at Doncaster.

3404

Doncaster 972.

To traffic 5/1902.

REPAIRS:
Don. ?/?—7/09.**G.**
Don. ?/?—17/10/14.**G.**
Don. 10/10/19—7/2/20.**G.**
Don. 16/5—8/9/23.**G.**
Don. 12/3—26/6/26.**G.**

BOILERS:
1397.
1402 ?/7/09.
1397 *(superheated)* 17/10/14.
7836 26/6/26.

SHEDS:
New England.
Boston 2/7/28.
New England 30/8/28.

RENUMBERED:
404N 8/9/23.
3404 30/3/25.

CONDEMNED: 26/4/29.
Cut up at Doncaster.

3405

Doncaster 965.

To traffic 4/1902.

REPAIRS:
Don. ?/?—3/10.**G.**
Don. ?/?—28/9/11.**G.**

Rebuilt to Q2.
Don. 11/3—12/6/20.**G.**
Don. 24/9/23—31/1/24.**G.**
Don. 19/5—31/12/27.**G.**
Don. 11/5—15/6/29.**G.**
Don. 19/3—23/4/32.**G.**

BOILERS:
1394.
1538 ?/3/10.
1393 *(superheated)* 28/9/11.
8050 31/12/27.

SHED:
Ardsley.

RENUMBERED:
405N 31/1/24.
3405 31/12/27.

CONDEMNED: 26/6/35.
Cut up at Doncaster.

3406

Doncaster 966.

To traffic 4/1902.

REPAIRS:
Don. ?/?—26/7/12.**G.**
Rebuilt to Q2.
Don. 20/7—28/11/23.**G.**
Don. 14/9/27—19/1/28.**G.**
Don. 8/11—6/12/30.**G.**

BOILERS:
1395.
7136 *(superheated)* 26/7/12.
8051 19/1/28.

SHED:
Ardsley.

RENUMBERED:
406N 28/11/23.
3406 19/1/28.

CONDEMNED: 3/2/34.
Cut up at Doncaster.

3407

Doncaster 967.

To traffic 4/1902.

REPAIRS:
Don. ?/?—4/10.**G.**
Don. ?/?—23/7/12.**G.**

Rebuilt to Q2.
Don. 7/7—1/11/19.**G.**
Don. 24/9/23—11/1/24.**G.**
Don. 2/7—22/8/24.**L.**
Don. 29/9—2/11/28.**G.**
Don. 13/6—18/7/31.**G.**

BOILERS:
1396.
1399 ?/4/10.
7135 *(superheated)* 23/7/12.
8088 2/11/28.

SHED:
Ardsley.

RENUMBERED:
407N 11/1/24.
3407 2/11/28.

CONDEMNED: 16/6/34.
Cut up at Doncaster.

3408

Doncaster 969.

To traffic 7/1902.

REPAIRS:
Don. ?/?—3/09.**G.**
Don. ?/?—18/8/16.**G.**
Don. 17/8/21—25/2/22.**G.**
Don. 9/7—8/11/24.**G.**

BOILERS:
1398.
1574 ?/3/09.
1540 *(superheated)* 18/8/16.

SHED:
Colwick.

RENUMBERED:
3408 8/11/24.

CONDEMNED: 2/9/27.
Cut up at Doncaster.

3409

Doncaster 970.

To traffic 6/1902.

REPAIRS:
Don. ?/?—4/10.**G.**
Don. ?/?—20/11/14.**G.**
Don. 11/7—13/10/23.**G.**
Don. 8/3—26/6/26.**G.**

Five further engines, Nos.441 to 445, were built between December 1906 and January 1907 and another five, Nos.446 to 450, were built in July and August 1909 similar to previous batches. All ten were built at Doncaster and were superheated from December 1912 to January 1919. Nos.442, 443, 444 and 448 had twin anti-vacuum valves but beginning with No.445 in September 1913 a single 4in. diameter valve became standard, and by Grouping had supplanted the earlier twin valves.

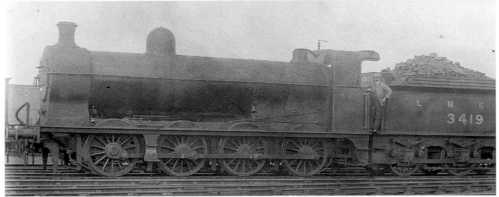

Only eight were never superheated, these being Nos.413N, 3419, 3428, 3431, 3433, 3434, 3437 and 3439. No.3431, withdrawn 28th November 1931 was the last survivor.

When Gresley had No.415 superheated in March 1912 it kept its balanced slide valve cylinder and special attention was given to lubrication. Results were good enough for the next ten, Nos.403, 422, 425, 427, 432, 435, 440, 442, 443 and 444, to be done similarly, and these were all fitted with Schmidt type superheaters, which only Nos.3422, 3425, 3435 and 3443 kept to withdrawal.

3409 cont./
Don. 8/12/28—19/1/29.**G.**

BOILERS:
1399.
1564 ?/4/10.
1544 *(superheated)* 20/11/14.
7835 26/6/26.

SHED:
Colwick.

RENUMBERED:
409ₙ 13/10/23.
3409 26/6/26.

CONDEMNED: 5/8/31.
Cut up at Doncaster.

3410

Doncaster 971.

To traffic 7/1902.

REPAIRS:
Don. ?/?—2/10.**G.**
Don. ?/?—12/6/12.**G.**
Rebuilt to Q2.
Don. 18/7—9/12/22.**G.**
Don. 6/2—4/7/25.**G.**
Don. 31/3—31/8/27.**G.**
Don. 5/10—2/11/29.**G.**
Don. 14/5—11/6/32.**G.**

BOILERS:
1400.
1546 ?/2/10.
7134 *(superheated)* 12/6/12.

SHEDS:
Colwick.
Ardsley 10/8/32.

RENUMBERED:
3410 4/7/25.

CONDEMNED: 18/10/35.
Cut up at Doncaster.

3411

Doncaster 973.

To traffic 7/1902.

REPAIRS:
Don. ?/?—4/11.**G.**
Don. 8/3—27/8/19.**G.**
Don. 15/11/23—1/3/24.**G.**

Don. 25/7—23/8/24.**L.**
Don. 8/2—1/5/26.**G.**
Don. 12/11/27—28/1/28.**G.**

BOILERS:
1401.
1394 ?/4/11.
1575 *(superheated)* 27/8/19.
1487 1/3/24.
7734 28/1/28.

SHED:
Colwick.

RENUMBERED:
3411 1/3/24.

CONDEMNED: 8/12/30.
Cut up at Doncaster.

3412

Doncaster 976.

To traffic 8/1902.

REPAIRS:
Don. ?/?—5/09.**G.**
Don. ?/?—3/12.**G.**
Don. ?/?—24/3/17.**G.**
Don. 3/10/22—3/2/23.**G.**
Don. 3/6—19/9/25.**G.**

BOILERS:
1402.
1404 ?/5/09.
1553 ?/3/12.
1567 *(superheated)* 24/3/17.

SHED:
Colwick.

RENUMBERED:
3412 19/9/25.

CONDEMNED: 23/7/28.
Cut up at Doncaster.

(3)413

Doncaster 982.

To traffic 9/1902.

REPAIRS:
Don. ?/?—4/14.**G.**
Don. 26/7—8/11/19.**G.**
Don. 15/8—28/11/23.**G.**

BOILERS:
1403.
1557 ?/4/14.

SHED:
Ardsley.

RENUMBERED:
413ₙ 28/11/23.

CONDEMNED: 16/5/27.
Cut up at Doncaster.

3414

Doncaster 978.

To traffic 9/1902.

REPAIRS:
Don. ?/?—2/09.**G.**
Don. ?/?—4/14.**G.**
Don. 22/4—20/11/20.**G.**
Don. 13/5—11/10/24.**G.**
Don. 5/2—26/11/27.**G.**

BOILERS:
1404.
1410 ?/2/09.
1398 ?/4/14.
7342 *(superheated)* 20/11/20.
8047 *(new)* 26/11/27.

SHED:
Colwick.

RENUMBERED:
3414 11/10/24.

CONDEMNED: 31/12/29.
Cut up at Doncaster.

3415

Doncaster 983.

To traffic 10/1902.

REPAIRS:
Don. ?/?—8/3/12.**G.**
Don. 21/9—27/11/20.**G.**
Don. 4/10/23—9/2/24.**G.**
Don. 14/7/26—18/1/27.**G.**

BOILERS:
1406.
7132 *(superheated)* 8/3/12.
7199 18/1/27.

SHED:
Colwick.

RENUMBERED:
3415 9/2/24.

CONDEMNED: 18/5/29.
Cut up at Doncaster.

3416

Doncaster 985.

To traffic 12/1902.

REPAIRS:
Don. ?/?—19/8/11.**G.**
Rebuilt to Q2.
Don. 2/12/20—30/4/21.**G.**
Don. 30/4—26/9/24.**G.**
Don. 11/11/26—5/2/27.**G.**
Don. 10/8—21/9/29.**G.**
Don. 19/11—17/12/32.**G.**

BOILERS:
1409.
1542 *(superheated)* 19/8/11.
7132 5/2/27.

SHED:
Colwick.

RENUMBERED:
3416 26/9/24.

CONDEMNED: 17/12/35.
Cut up at Doncaster.

3417

Doncaster 984.

To traffic 1/1903.

REPAIRS:
Don. ?/?—2/12/08.**G.**
Rebuilt to Q2.
Don. 28/10/20—12/3/21.**G.**
Don. 30/10/23—15/3/24.**G.**
Don. 25/5—6/11/26.**G.**
Don. 28/9—26/10/29.**G.**
Don. 28/1—25/2/33.**G.**

BOILERS:
1405.
1577 *(superheated)* 2/12/08.
7341 12/3/21.
989 15/3/24.
7194 6/11/26.
7835 25/2/33.

WORKS CODES:- Cw - Cowlairs. Dar- Darlington. Don - Doncaster. Ghd - Gateshead. Gor - Gorton. Inv - Inverurie. Str - Stratford.
REPAIR CODES:- **C/H** - Casual Heavy. **C/L** - Casual Light. **G** - General. **H**- Heavy. **H/I** - Heavy Intermediate. **L** - Light. **L/I** - Light Intermediate. **N/C** - Non-Classified.

In July 1914 Gresley decided against buying any more Schmidt type superheaters and from then on the Robinson type became standard. No.409 got its Robinson type when it was superheated in November 1914, but there was no external difference to distinguish which type was fitted. Under the LNER seven, Nos.3415 (18/1/27); 3427 (29/5/25); 3432 (16/2/29); 3440 (13/10/28); 3442 (2/7/27) and 3444 (11/5/29), were changed from Schmidt to Robinson type. Nos.401 to 421 had taper shank buffers and Nos.3409, 3411 and 3418 still had that type in LNER livery.

The normal smokebox door was of relatively small diameter with a cross rail below the upper hinge strap. Nos.422 to 450 had parallel case buffers and most of the earlier engines later changed to that type.

In 1914 Gresley devised a twin-tube superheater, and three Q1 were fitted with them: 450 (December 1915); 408 (August 1916) and 447 (February 1917). No.450 was rebuilt to Q2 class in October 1920 and No.447 had its superheater changed to Robinson type when ex works 30th March 1925 as No.3447. No.3408 still had twin-tube to its 2nd September 1927 withdrawal, and was an oddity in having a 4ft 9in. diameter smokebox door instead of the usual 3ft 11¾in. type.

By LNER days most had the door cross rail moved to a position above the upper hinge strap. No.3430 was last ex works 26th January 1928 and is seen here on 13th October 1931, ten days after withdrawal. Its chimney was the usual 2ft 2¼in. built-up type, which gave a height from rail of 13ft 4⅛in.

No attempt was made to bring any within the LNER 13ft 0in. Load Gauge, but at least two, Nos.3427 and 3435 acquired a 2in. shorter, plain chimney when they were superheated in October and November 1912. They kept these chimneys to withdrawal. All had, and kept, four Ramsbottom type safety valves, until five new boilers were put to work from November 1927 (see page 19).

When superheater was put in, the cylinder pistons were given tail rods, and these, with the flat platform cover for them, needed a 9in. frame extension at the front.

The tail rod usually survived to withdrawal but two were noted as having them removed, No.3414 from 11th October 1924 and 3442 from 16th July 1925. The tender is an early Class B type carrying 5 tons of coal and 3670 gallons of water. By LNER take-over all modern tenders had been taken for use with classes O1 and O2.

This is also an early Class B tender but from one of the batches provided with a grab handle at the front end. Note that classification has been applied to the bufferbeam; this was done at Darlington, which gave general repairs to Nos.3447 (30/3/25); 3424 (27/5/25); 3427 (29/5/25); 3442 (16/7/25); 3429 (31/7/25) and 3432 (6/8/25).

3417 cont./
SHED:
Colwick.

RENUMBERED:
3417 15/3/24.

CONDEMNED: 17/12/35.
Cut up at Doncaster.

3418

Doncaster 986.

To traffic 1/1903.

REPAIRS:
Don. ?/?—8/12/14.**G**.
Don. 22/10/20—19/3/21.**G**.
Don. 12/3—16/8/24.**G**.
Don. 8/1—7/10/27.**G**.

BOILERS:
1408.
1410 *(superheated)* 8/12/14.
7348 19/3/21.
 986 16/8/24.
7133 7/10/27.

SHED:
Colwick.

RENUMBERED:
3418 16/8/24.

CONDEMNED: 30/11/29.
Cut up at Doncaster.

3419

Doncaster 987.

To traffic 1/1903.

REPAIRS:
Don. ?/?—9/09.**G**.
Don. ?/?—12/13.**G**.
Don. 25/3—26/8/22.**G**.
Don. 16/4—18/7/25.**G**.

BOILERS:
1407.
1397 ?/9/09.
1546 ?/12/13.

SHED:
Ardsley.

RENUMBERED:
3419 18/7/25.

CONDEMNED: 13/9/28.
Cut up at Doncaster.

3420

Doncaster 988.

To traffic 1/1903.

REPAIRS:
Don. ?/?—7/09.**G**.
Don. ?/?—5/9/11.**G**.
Rebuilt to Q2.
Don. 16/9/13—14/2/14.**G**.
Rebuilt to Q3.
Don. 3/10/24—22/1/25.**G**.
Don. 10/12/25—2/1/26.**L**.
Don. 2/3—13/5/27.**L**.
Don. 19/10—16/11/29.**G**.
Don. 10/2—3/3/34.**G**.

BOILERS:
1411.
1398 ?/7/09.
1537 *(superheated)* 5/9/11.
7250 14/2/14.
7252 16/11/29.

SHEDS:
New England.
Ardsley 15/2/25.

RENUMBERED:
3420 22/1/25.

CONDEMNED: 10/2/37.
Cut up at Doncaster.

3421

Doncaster 989.

To traffic 1/1903.

REPAIRS:
Don. ?/?—12/08.**G**.
Don. ?/?—23/12/15.**G**.
Rebuilt to Q2.
Don. 13/2—24/4/20.**G**.
Don. 31/7—22/11/23.**G**.
Don. 22/3—17/7/26.**G**.
Don. 9/2—16/3/29.**G**.
Don. 8/8—19/9/31.**G**.

BOILERS:
1410.
1405 ?/12/08.
1537 *(superheated)* 23/12/15.
7138 17/7/26.
8175 19/9/31.

SHED:
Colwick.

RENUMBERED:
421$_N$ 22/11/23.
3421 15/4/25.

CONDEMNED: 19/5/34.
Cut up at Doncaster.

3422

Doncaster 1008.

To traffic 8/1903.

REPAIRS:
Don. ?/?—24/12/12.**G**.
Don. 27/9/22—21/3/23.**G**.
Don. 1/5—1/8/25.**G**.

BOILERS:
1539.
7140 *(superheated)* 24/12/12.

SHED:
New England.

RENUMBERED:
3422 1/8/25.

CONDEMNED: 1/8/28.
Cut up at Doncaster.

3423

Doncaster 1007.

To traffic 7/1903.

REPAIRS:
Don. ?/?—11/09.**G**.
Don. ?/?—6/5/15.**G**.
Don. 7/3—16/6/23.**G**.
Don. 17/8—31/10/25.**G**.

BOILERS:
1538.
1411 ?/11/09.
1403 *(superheated)* 6/5/15.

SHEDS:
New England.
Colwick ?/?

RENUMBERED:
3423 31/1/25.

CONDEMNED: 27/6/28.
Cut up at Doncaster.

3424

Doncaster 1010.

To traffic 6/1903.

REPAIRS:
Don. ?/?—4/6/15.**G**.
Don. 14/2—17/6/22.**G**.
Dar. 12/12/24—27/5/25.**G**.
Don. 17—27/8/25.**L**.

BOILERS:
1540.
1402 *(superheated)* 4/6/15.
7734 27/5/25.

SHED:
New England.

RENUMBERED:
3424 27/5/25.

CONDEMNED: 10/10/27.
Cut up at Doncaster.

3425

Doncaster 1009.

To traffic 9/1903.

REPAIRS:
Don. ?/?—1/11.**G**.
Don. ?/?—14/6/13.**G**.
Don. 27/9/22—13/1/23.**G**.
Don. 26/6—24/10/25.**G**.

BOILERS:
1542.
1543 ?/1/11.
7196 *(superheated)* 14/6/13.

SHED:
Colwick.

RENUMBERED:
3425 *by* 2/25.

CONDEMNED: 27/6/28.
Cut up at Doncaster.

WORKS CODES:- Cw - Cowlairs. Dar- Darlington. Don - Doncaster. Ghd - Gateshead. Gor - Gorton. Inv - Inverurie. Str - Stratford.
REPAIR CODES:- **C/H** - Casual Heavy. **C/L** - Casual Light. **G** - General. **H**- Heavy. **H/I** - Heavy Intermediate. **L** - Light. **L/I** - Light Intermediate. **N/C** - Non-Classified.

No.420, built new in January 1903 at Doncaster, was just the same as Nos.402 to 421 of the same batch until it went to works in 1911. Ex works on the 5th September it had a Schmidt superheater and boiler pitched 2in. higher. It also had piston valves and cylinders with piston tail rods and the corresponding 9 inch frame extension. It was then similar to those which became Class Q2, until it went to works again on 16th September 1913. Ex works 14th February 1914, No.420 had been fitted with a 5ft 6in. diameter boiler and 24-element Robinson superheater as used by those which became LNER Class K2 (*see* Volume 18). It was in grey paint without lining and had substantial packing plates to support the firebox extension brackets. The new cab had shaped windows and was 8ft 0in. instead of 7ft 1in. wide inside. Other changes were to fluted rods, parallel shank buffers, removal of safety chains, top lamp iron and cross rail above hinge strap.

By Grouping the only significant change to No.420 was the tender because it then had one of the more modern Class B with the 6½ tons coal capacity and 3500 gallons of water. Axles were spaced at 6ft 10½in. and 6ft 1½in. apart. It had this tender until it went for repair on 3rd October 1924.

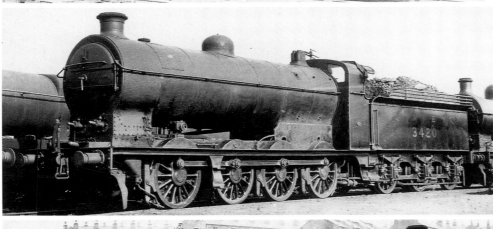

Ex works 22nd January 1925, as LNER 3420, it was in black with single red lining which it kept to 19th October 1929. The tender had been changed to a Stirling Class D, built in May 1892, which it then kept until withdrawal.

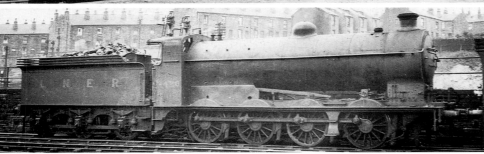

Out 16th November 1929, the boiler had been changed to another one built in 1914 but which now had Ross 'pop' safety valves. The number had moved to the cab where only 7½in. figures could be used but the LNER on the tender was increased to 12in. high letters; painting was black unlined. It had a general repair in March 1934 but was withdrawn 10th February 1937 making Class Q3 extinct and it was also the last exGNR 0-8-0.

Latterly quite a number were coupled with Stirling design tenders of class D, having three coal rails, tank with square corners and wood bufferbeam at the rear end. In LNER painting Nos.3401, 3403, 3408, 3409, 3419, 3444, 3448 and 3449 are known to have had this type. No.3401 is of particular interest because its brake standpipe carries two load class collars, D in the GNR scheme, and 5 in the 1924 LNER Southern Area list.

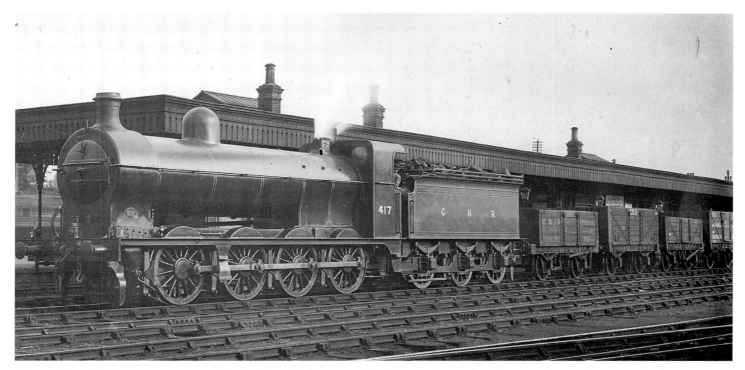

Although No.401 came out new painted black with red lining and polished brass rims to the splashers, all the other forty-nine first had green lined livery. Note tender front has a cut-out but no grab rail.

Only No.401 had brass rims on the splashers and, although painted over later, they were still there at withdrawal (*see* page 15, top). Until December 1912 the others - and No.401 from February 1906 - had this two-tone green painting with broad black and narrow white lining.

From 2nd December 1912, Gresley decided that goods and shunting engines should be painted dark grey without lining, to save about £1000 a year. Numbers and letters became white but still had shading. All Q1's were in this style at Grouping.

CLASS Q 1

3426

Doncaster 1011.

To traffic 9/1903.

REPAIRS:
Don. ?/?—10/10.**G**.
Don. ?/?—11/12.**G**.
Don. ?/?—6/11/15.**G**.
Don. 5/8—10/12/21.**G**.
Don. 24/10/24—31/1/25.**G**.
Don. 18/12/25—27/2/26.**L**.
Don. 26/1—9/3/29.**G**.

BOILERS:
1537.
1400 10/10.
1407 11/12.
1405 *(superheated)* 6/11/15.
8174 *(new)* 9/3/29.

SHEDS:
New England.
Bradford ?/?
Colwick 9/3/29.

RENUMBERED:
3426 31/1/25.

CONDEMNED: 9/9/31.
Cut up at Doncaster.

3427

Doncaster 1012.

To traffic 9/1903.

REPAIRS:
Don. ?/?—10/08.**G**.
Don. ?/?—19/10/12.**G**.
Don. 25/8—17/12/21.**G**.
Dar. 12/12/24—29/5/25.**G**.

BOILERS:
1543.
 401 10/08.
7137 *(superheated)* 19/10/12.
1410 17/12/21.
7735 29/5/25.

SHED:
New England.

RENUMBERED:
3427 29/5/25.

CONDEMNED: 11/4/29.
Cut up at Doncaster.

3428

Doncaster 1015.

To traffic 9/1903.

REPAIRS:
Don. ?/?—9/08.**G**.
Don. ?/?—1/16.**G**.
Don. 4/3—13/8/21.**G**.
Don. 11/1—8/3/24.**G**.

BOILERS:
1541.
1562 ?/9/08.
6969 ?/1/16.

SHED:
Ardsley.

RENUMBERED:
3428 8/3/24.

CONDEMNED: 10/4/26.
Cut up at Doncaster.

3429

Doncaster 1013.

To traffic 9/1903.

REPAIRS:
Don. ?/?—7/09.**G**.
Don. ?/?—5/3/14.**G**.
Don. 24/2—24/6/22.**G**.
Dar. 12/1—31/7/25.**G**.
Don. 29/8—11/10/28.**G**.

BOILERS:
1544.
1541 ?/7/09.
7201 *(superheated)* 5/3/14.

SHEDS:
New England.
Hitchin 11/10/28.

RENUMBERED:
3429 31/7/25.

CONDEMNED: 6/12/30.
Cut up at Doncaster.

3430

Doncaster 1014.

To traffic 9/1903.

REPAIRS:
Don. ?/?—10/11.**G**.
Don. ?/?—4/4/14.**G**.
Don. 22/9/21—18/2/22.**G**.
Don. 11/10/24—24/1/25.**G**.
Don. 21/10/27—26/1/28.**G**.

BOILERS:
1545.
1401 ?/10/11.
7203 *(superheated)* 4/4/14.
1547 24/1/25.

SHEDS:
New England.
Bradford ?/?

RENUMBERED:
3430 24/1/25.

CONDEMNED: 3/10/31.
Cut up at Doncaster.

3431

Doncaster 1016.

To traffic 10/1903.

REPAIRS:
Don. ?/?—12/09.**G**.
Don. ?/?—11/13.**G**.
Don. 16/6—21/10/22.**G**.
Don. 27/8—6/12/24.**G**.
Don. 12/6—3/8/28.**G**.

BOILERS:
1546.
1544 ?/12/09.
1545 ?/11/13.
1392 6/12/24.

SHEDS:
New England.
Ardsley ?/?

RENUMBERED:
3431 6/12/24.

CONDEMNED: 28/11/31.
Cut up at Doncaster.

3432

Doncaster 1027.

To traffic 1/1904.

REPAIRS:
Don. ?/?—8/10.**G**.
Don. ?/?—13/11/12.**G**.
Don. 14/2—1/7/22.**G**.
Dar. 17/12/24—6/8/25.**G**.
Don. 18—29/8/25.**L**.
Don. 12/1—16/2/29.**G**.

BOILERS:
1553.
1396 ?/8/10.
7139 *(superheated)* 13/11/12.
8173 *(new)* 16/2/29.

SHEDS:
New England.
Colwick 16/2/29.

RENUMBERED:
3432 6/8/25.

CONDEMNED: 27/10/31.
Cut up at Doncaster.

3433

Doncaster 1028.

To traffic 3/1904.

REPAIRS:
Don. ?/?—12/09.**G**.
Don. ?/?—6/16.**G**.
Don. 4/5—17/9/21.**G**.
Don. 31/7—29/11/24.**G**.
Don. 11/10/26—19/3/27.**G**.

BOILERS:
1551.
1567 ?/12/09.
1571 ?/6/16.

SHEDS:
Colwick.
Ardsley ?/?

RENUMBERED:
3433 29/11/24.

CONDEMNED: 8/2/30.
Cut up at Doncaster.

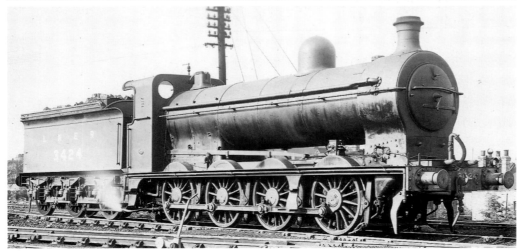

(above) **From February 1923, Group livery for this class became black with single red lining, and the first four included the ampersand in the new company's initials. They were Nos.412 (3/2/23); 443 (10/3/23), 422 (21/3/23) and 449 (28/4/23).**

(left) **The ampersand was then discarded and the next three had this style, Nos.403 (2/6/23); 423 (16/6/23) and 440 (4/8/23). They were followed by four in the same style but with the N suffix to the number: 404N (8/9/23); 409N (13/10/23); 413N (28/11/23) and 448N (7/2/24).**

Beginning with No.3415, ex works 9th February 1924, all got full LNER number and continued to have red lining until the 1928 painting economies took effect. By the end of 1928 thirteen had been withdrawn, and another ten in 1929; all these retained red lining.

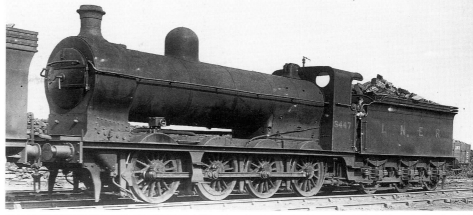

From March 1929 the number was moved to the cab side, where only 7½in. figures could be used, but tender letters then became 12in. instead of 7½in. Only two survived to have this alteration: 3444 (11/5/29) and 3447 (25/4/31). When No.3447 was withdrawn on 18th October 1935 Class Q1 was then extinct.

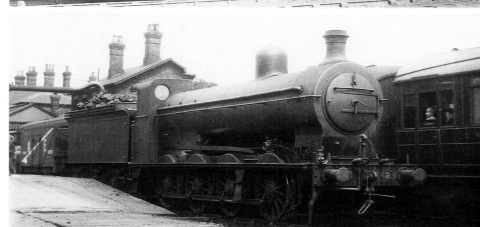

Ex works 9th March 1929, No.3426 just missed the move to cab number but it was one of the five to get a new boiler which had Ross 'pop' safety valves. The other four engines were: 3414 (26/11/27); 3401 (15/12/27); 3446 (27/7/28) and 3432 (16/2/29).

This curious arrangement of sandboxes combined with the leading splasher seems to have been fitted only to No.404. It is a pre-1913 photograph but the front buffers have already been changed from taper to parallel shank type, but it still has plain coupling rods. These sandboxes were fitted in August 1909 when a trial of gravity instead of steam application was made.

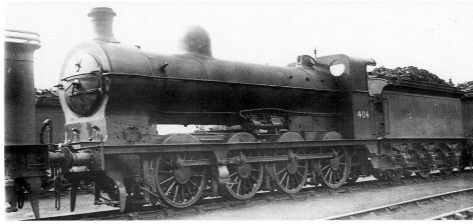

In June 1917 No.404 was the subject of an experiment with a Willans type feed water heater combined with a Worthington pump. Date of removal has not been found, but would be either when it went for repair in May 1923 or in March 1926.

3434

Doncaster 1029.

To traffic 3/1904.

REPAIRS:
Don. ?/?—1/13.**G.**
Don. 23/5—22/10/21.**G.**
Don. 10/1—16/5/25.**G.**

BOILERS:
1555.
1399 ?/1/13.

SHEDS:
New England.
Hornsey by 5/26.
Hitchin 18/1/28.

RENUMBERED:
3434 16/5/25.

CONDEMNED: 27/6/28.
Cut up at Doncaster.

3435

Doncaster 1050.

To traffic 3/1904.

REPAIRS:
Don. ?/?—11/11/12.**G.**
Don. 7/1—13/5/22.**G.**
Don. 8/1—23/5/25.**G.**

BOILERS:
1552.
7138 (superheated) 11/11/12.
 983 23/5/25.

SHEDS:
New England.
Hornsey by 5/26.

RENUMBERED:
3435 23/5/25.

CONDEMNED: 17/5/29.
Cut up at Doncaster.

3436

Doncaster 1051.

To traffic 3/1904.

REPAIRS:
Don. ?/?—29/1/20.**G.**
Don. 16/6—28/10/22.**G.**
Don. 15/1—25/4/25.**G.**
Don. 17/11/27—2/2/28.**G.**

BOILERS:
1548.
1396 (superheated) 29/1/20.

SHED:
Colwick.

RENUMBERED:
3436 25/4/25.

CONDEMNED: 8/2/30.
Cut up at Doncaster.

3437

Doncaster 1052.

To traffic 4/1904.

REPAIRS:
Don. ?/?—12/14.**G.**
Don. 29/8—17/12/21.**G.**
Don. 15/9—13/12/24.**G.**

BOILERS:
1549.
1560 ?/12/14.
1543 13/12/24.

SHEDS:
Colwick.
Ardsley ?/?

RENUMBERED:
3437 13/12/24.

CONDEMNED: 1/3/28.
Cut up at Doncaster.

3438

Doncaster 1053.

To traffic 8/1904.

REPAIRS:
Don. ?/?—24/3/17.**G.**
Don. 30/8—23/12/22.**G.**
Don. 15/7—31/10/25.**G.**

BOILERS:
1550.
7349 (superheated) 24/3/17.

SHEDS:
Doncaster.
Ardsley ?/?

RENUMBERED:
3438 31/10/25.

CONDEMNED: 17/5/29.
Cut up at Doncaster.

3439

Doncaster 1054.

To traffic 8/1904.

REPAIRS:
Don. ?/?—24/3/17.**G.**
Don. 15/3—3/9/21.**G.**
Don. 1/10/24—17/1/25.**G.**

BOILERS:
1547.
1553 24/3/17.
1561 17/1/25.

SHEDS:
Colwick.
Ardsley 22/9/25.

RENUMBERED:
3439 17/1/25.

CONDEMNED: 9/2/27.
Cut up at Doncaster.

3440

Doncaster 1055.

To traffic 9/1904.

REPAIRS:
Don. ?/?—8/8/13.**G.**
Don. 3/5—4/8/23.**G.**
Don. 16/11/25—27/2/26.**G.**
Don. 29/8—13/10/28.**G.**

BOILERS:
1554.
7197 (superheated) 8/8/13.
7832 27/2/26.

SHEDS:
New England.
Colwick ?/?

RENUMBERED:
3440 by 7/25.

CONDEMNED: 28/11/31.
Cut up at Doncaster.

3441

Doncaster 1139.

To traffic 12/1906.

REPAIRS:
Don. ?/?—25/1/19.**G.**
Don. 29/4—15/10/21.**G.**
Don. 16/9/24—15/1/25.**G.**
Don. 6—21/7/25.**L.**
Don. 29/12/28—9/2/29.**G.**

BOILERS:
1575.
7345 (superheated) 25/1/19.

SHEDS:
New England.
Ardsley by 16/9/28.

RENUMBERED:
3441 15/1/25.

CONDEMNED: 11/6/30.
Cut up at Doncaster.

3442

Doncaster 1140.

To traffic 1/1907.

REPAIRS:
Don. ?/?—14/6/13.**G.**
Don. 19/7—2/12/22.**G.**
Dar. 2/12/24—16/7/25.**G.**
Don. 25/4—2/7/27.**G.**

BOILERS:
1568.
7195 (superheated) 14/6/13.

SHEDS:
New England.
Ardsley ?/?

RENUMBERED:
3442 16/7/25.

CONDEMNED: 27/9/30.
Cut up at Doncaster.

3443

Doncaster 1141.

To traffic 12/1906.

REPAIRS:
Don. ?/?—4/12/12.**G.**
Don. 25/7/22—10/3/23.**G.**
Don. 4/1—20/3/26.**G.**

BOILERS:
1576.
7141 (superheated) 4/12/12.
1569 10/3/23.

SHED:
Colwick.

RENUMBERED:
3443 20/3/26.

CONDEMNED: 2/1/29.
Cut up at Doncaster.

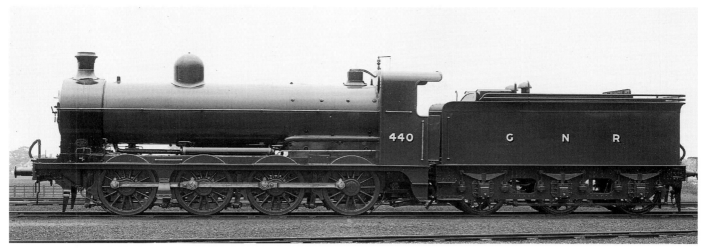

In August 1912 No.439, and in July 1913 No.440 were fitted with a Weir feed water heater and pump, but both had lost this equipment before the LNER took them over. It was removed from No.440 in April 1920, and (probably) from No.439 in September 1921.

3444

Doncaster 1142.

To traffic 12/1906.

REPAIRS:
Don. ?/?—8/8/13.**G.**
Don. 11/10/22—27/1/23.**G.**
Don. 3/7—10/10/25.**G.**
Don. 6/4—11/5/29.**G.**

BOILERS:
1571.
7198 *(superheated)* 8/8/13.
7203 10/10/25.

SHED:
Ardsley.

RENUMBERED:
3444 10/10/25.

CONDEMNED: 12/7/32.
Cut up at Doncaster.

3445

Doncaster 1143.

To traffic 12/1906.

REPAIRS:
Don. ?/?—19/9/13.**G.**
Don. 30/3—1/10/21.**G.**
Don. 5/12/24—25/4/25.**G.**

BOILERS:
1569.
1555 *(superheated)* 19/9/13.

SHEDS:
Ardsley.
Doncaster ?/?
Ardsley 25/4/25.

RENUMBERED:
3445 25/4/25.

CONDEMNED: 27/6/28.
Cut up at Doncaster.

3446

Doncaster 1236.

To traffic 7/1909.

REPAIRS:
Don. ?/?—18/2/14.**G.**
Don. 11/3—28/5/21.**G.**
Don. 29/11/23—29/3/24.**G.**
Don. 21/4—21/8/26.**G.**
Don. 6/3—27/7/28.**G.**
BOILERS:
6965.
7200 *(superheated)* 18/2/14.
8085 *(new)* 27/7/28.

SHEDS:
New England.
Ardsley *by* 16/9/28.

RENUMBERED:
3446 29/3/24.

CONDEMNED: 27/2/32.
Cut up at Doncaster.

3447

Doncaster 1237.

To traffic 7/1909.

REPAIRS:
Don. ?/?—17/2/17.**G.**
Don. 11/8/21—18/3/22.**G.**
Dar. 19/11/24—30/3/25.**G.**
Don. 10/8—18/11/27.**G.**
Don. 21/3—25/4/31.**G.**

BOILERS:
6966.
1411 *(superheated)* 17/2/17.
7733 30/3/25.

SHEDS:
New England.
Hitchin 5/9/25.
Ardsley 17/10/29.

RENUMBERED:
3447 30/3/25.

CONDEMNED: 18/10/35.
Cut up at Doncaster.

3448

Doncaster 1238.

To traffic 7/1909.

REPAIRS:
Don. ?/?—15/1/14.**G.**
Don. 31/8—20/11/20.**G.**
Don. 4/10/23—7/2/24.**G.**
Don. 26/4—30/10/26.**G.**
Don. 26/1—9/3/29.**G.**

BOILERS:
6967.
7199 *(superheated)* 15/1/14.
7197 30/10/26.

SHED:
Colwick.
RENUMBERED:
448N 7/2/24.
3448 8/5/25.

CONDEMNED: 12/2/32.
Cut up at Doncaster.

3449

Doncaster 1239.

To traffic 8/1909.

REPAIRS:
Don. ?/?—14/2/14.**G.**
Don. 8/1—28/4/23.**G.**
Don. 16/6—3/10/25.**G.**
Don. 17/1—5/4/28.**G.**

BOILERS:
6968.
7202 *(superheated)* 14/2/14.
1482 28/4/23.

SHED:
Colwick.

RENUMBERED:
3449 3/10/25.

CONDEMNED: 27/8/30.
Cut up at Doncaster.

From September to November 1909 Doncaster built five new engines, Nos.451 to 455 as No.417 but fitted with exhaust steam injector. Their steam chest was 2in. higher as was the boiler centre and so they were fitted with 2in. shorter chimney of the plain type. This maintained height from rail level to top of chimney at 13ft. 4⅛in.

No more new Q2 were built but Gresley made further conversions from Q1 class. In August and September 1911 Nos.405, 416 and 420 were fitted similarly to Nos.451 to 455 but when No.402 was rebuilt in April 1912 it was fitted with a Robinson superheater.

(opposite) On the ten engines so far made Q2, anti-vacuum valves were fitted at the base of the smokebox, but they also had dampers which closed automatically when steam was shut off, so as to prevent heat damage to the elements. No.410 with Schmidt superheater was added to this class in June 1912 but by May 1913, it was found that dampers could be discarded and they were then removed.

CLASS Q 2

3450

Doncaster 1240.

To traffic 8/1909.

REPAIRS:
Don. ?/?—11/12/15.**G.**
Don. 29/5—23/10/20.**G.**
Rebuilt to Q2.
Don. 4/6—25/10/24.**G.**
Don. 26/5—24/8/27.**G.**
Don. 1/3—5/4/30.**G.**

BOILERS:
6969.
1408 (*superheated*) 11/12/15.
8047 5/4/30.

SHED:
Colwick.

RENUMBERED:
3450 25/10/24.

CONDEMNED: 15/6/33.
Cut up at Doncaster.

3451

Doncaster 1241.

To traffic 9/1909.

REPAIRS:
Don. 1/7—16/10/20.**G.**
Don. 12/8—23/12/24.**G.**

Don. 6/5—6/8/27.**G.**
Don. 31/5—28/6/30.**G.**

BOILERS:
6970.
8049 28/6/30.

SHED:
Colwick.

RENUMBERED:
3451 23/12/24.

CONDEMNED: 30/9/33.
Cut up at Doncaster.

3452

Doncaster 1244.

To traffic 10/1909.

REPAIRS:
Don. 28/10/21—4/2/22.**G.**
Dar. 15/11/24—16/6/25.**G.**
Don. 2/3—20/4/29.**G.**
Don. 30/1—27/2/32.**G.**

BOILER:
6971.

SHEDS:
New England.
King's Cross 31/10/25.
New England 1/12/25.
Ardsley 18/4/29.

RENUMBERED:
3452 16/6/25.

CONDEMNED: 24/2/34.
Cut up at Doncaster.

3453

Doncaster 1245.

To traffic 10/1909.

REPAIRS:
Don. 29/1—1/5/20.**G.**
Don. 22/12/23—26/4/24.**G.**
Don. 20/4—25/5/29.**G.**

BOILERS:
6972.
1577 25/5/29.

SHEDS:
Doncaster *at* 12/23.
Ardsley ?/?

RENUMBERED:
3453 26/4/24.

CONDEMNED: 20/5/33.
Cut up at Doncaster.

3454

Doncaster 1248.

To traffic 11/1909.

REPAIRS:
Don. 9/7/22—27/1/23.**G.**
Don. 13/3—11/7/25.**G.**
Don. 15/3—25/10/27.**G.**
Don. 22/2—29/3/30.**G.**

BOILER:
6973.

SHEDS:
New England.
Ardsley *after* 23/2/23.

RENUMBERED:
3454 21/2/25.

CONDEMNED: 24/2/34.
Cut up at Doncaster.

3455

Doncaster 1250.

To traffic 11/1909.

REPAIRS:
Don. 18/2—29/5/20.**G.**
Don. 7/1—18/4/25.**G.**
Don. 6/7—17/8/29.**G.**
Don. 14/5—18/6/32.**G.**

BOILERS:
6974.
7349 17/8/29.
8173 18/6/32.

SHEDS:
Doncaster *at* 12/23.
Ardsley ?/?.

RENUMBERED:
3455 18/4/25.

CONDEMNED: 26/8/33.
Cut up at Doncaster.

Note: In the tables relating to Class Q2 above, the first engine dealt with is No.3450 which started life as a Q1 but was later rebuilt to Q2 standard in October 1920. The other engines in the table were all built as Q2's, with superheaters and piston valves.

No.453, new in October 1909 was one of the final batch of five 0-8-0's. Based on Q1, they differed by having a superheater, piston valves and a boiler pitched 2in. higher. They began working from New England on the coal trains to London and here at Greenwood is taking a full load to the Capital. On the Down Slow line a train of empties is making its way north back to the collieries.

(left) In July 1912 Nos.406 and 407 were rebuilt to Q2 and had anti-vacuum valves put on the header instead of at the base of the smokebox. Until August 1913 twin valves of 'pepperpot' type were used, but there was then a change to a single 4in. diameter which all had by 1919, and this remained as the standard type in LNER days.

(below) When No.420 moved on to Q3 class, its boiler with Schmidt superheater was used from December 1915 on No.421 which was then rebuilt with piston valve cylinder, higher pitched boiler, and shorter plain chimney.

One more addition was made to Q2 class - No.450 in October 1920. In December 1915 it had been fitted with a twin-tube superheater but kept its balanced slide valves. It kept the twin-tube type to March 1930 but in October 1920 it was fitted with piston valve cylinders like those in No.417 so that its boiler pitch was not raised. Nos.3417 and 3450 thus kept 8ft 4¼in. pitch whereas on the other twelve it was 8ft 6¼in.

Until December 1927 all were fitted with four Ramsbottom safety valves, and Nos.3416 and 3417, withdrawn on 17th December 1935, kept this type when they were last of class. Note that 3416 also kept original type of taper shank buffers, and the tall built-up type of chimney with deep rim.

Seven engines got replacement boilers, built from 1927 and which had two Ross 'pop' valves. These were Nos.3406 (19/1/28); 3407 (2/11/28); 3450 (5/4/30); 3451 (28/6/30); 3421 (19/9/31) and 3455 (18/6/32).

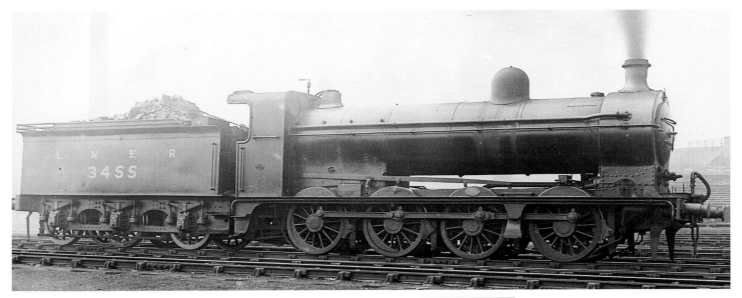

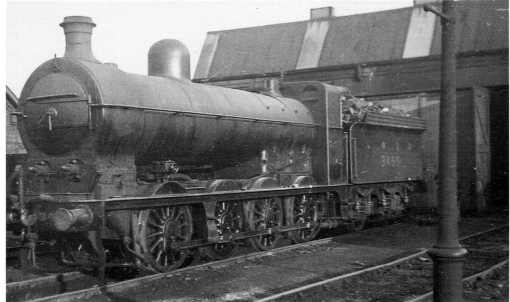

(above) **Curiously, all three types of chimney used on this class could be seen on a single engine. No.455 began with the 2ft 0¼in. tall plain type which it kept until after 1925. Note that at some time (April 1925 is likely) it had been fitted with a smokebox from a Q1 - shown by the lamp iron fixed on front plate - all other Q2's had them on the door.**

(left) **3455, still with number on tender although ex works 17th August 1929, then had a 2ft 2¼in. built-up chimney which would make its rim 13ft 6⅛in. from rail level. Note tender type had also changed to Class D, but the lamp iron was still on the smokebox front plate.**

Those 'shopped' from 1930 tended to have the chimney changed to the 1ft 11¼in. tall 'plantpot' type used by J6 class. No.3455 was so fitted ex works 18th June 1932. Note that the upper lamp iron was now fixed on the door, bringing the engine into line with the rest of the class.

A very late detail added was a stop to prevent the smokebox door swinging too far back. It was certainly fitted to Nos.3405 (23/4/32); 3417 (25/2/33) and 3455 (18/6/32). Nos.3410 (11/6/32) and 3452 (27/2/32) *may* have been so fitted, and 3416 (17/12/32) is a possibility.

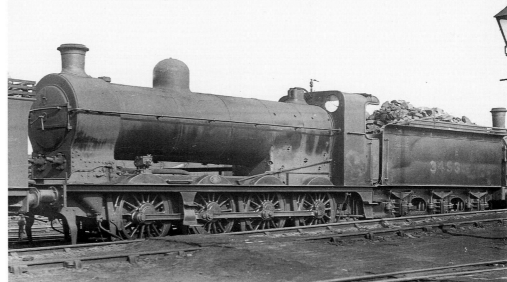

By LNER days Q2 class ranked low for tender type but some did still have the Ivatt early Class B coupled, but after 1930, only No.3405 had one of those.

(below) The others finished their careers coupled to 3-rail Stirling Class D tenders, except No.3407 which had an Ivatt Class A built in December 1897.

All began with green lined livery and except for Nos.421 and 450 had it as Q2 class. From December 1912 there was a steady change to dark grey without lining, and all were grey at Grouping.

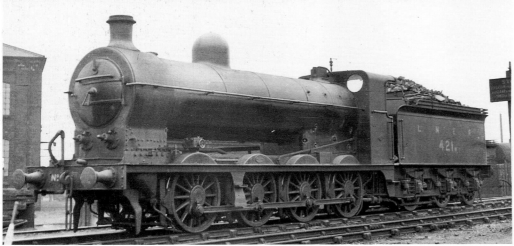

(centre) Ex works 27th January 1923, No.454 had plain tender sides but all the others duly got black paint with single red lining. First to carry LNER were: 405N (31/1/24); 406N (28/11/23); 407N (11/1/24) and 421N (22/11/23).

(below) No.3452 was the only Q2 repaired at Darlington and when ex works 16th June 1925, in line with their custom, its classification was shown on the buffer beam. They also used its GNR Class K1 and not LNER Class Q2. Note that its standpipe carries two load class collars; the GN Class D, and LNER Southern Area Class 6.

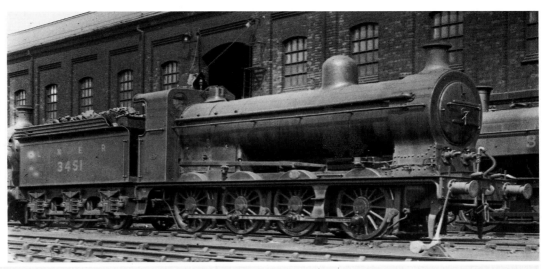

By April 1925 all those repaired at Doncaster had full LNER number in 12in. shaded transfers underneath 7½in. LNER letters, but at their first repair after June 1928 lining was no longer applied. Only No.3402, withdrawn 13th September 1927, did not go into unlined black.

(above) With the possible exception of No.3453, last ex works 25th May 1929, the other thirteen had number moved to the cab where only 7½in. figures could be used, but LNER on the tender then became 12in.

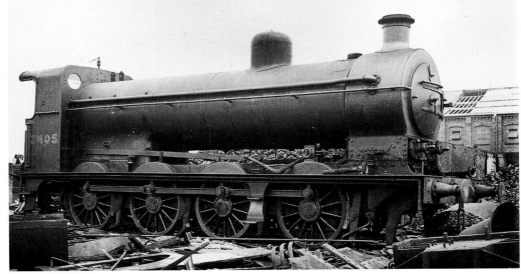

(right) No.3405 was withdrawn on 26th June 1935 followed on 18th October by 3410, and when both 3416 and 3417 were withdrawn on 17th December 1935, Class Q2 was extinct.

Thirty-three similar engines and tenders were built by Kitson & Co., Leeds between September 1903 and May 1904. these were numbered as followed: 56 to 59, 64, 65, 67, 68, 70, 71, 85, 86, 87, 91, 92, 135 to 140, and 142 to 153. Note parallel shank buffers with end collar and circular head.

Kitson & Co. built another five similar engines, Nos.1073 to 1077, during July and August 1905. These were the last ones built with the 3250 gallons tender.

CLASS Q 4

6052

Neilson Reid 6251.

To traffic 11/1902.

REPAIRS:
Gor. ?/?—?/1/07.**G.**
Gor. ?/?—4/1/08.**G.**
Gor. ?/?—25/11/11.**G.**
Gor. ?/?—30/6/17.**G.**
Gor. 15/4—5/8/22.**G.**
Gor. 12/7—1/11/24.**G.**
Gor. 26/2—16/4/27.**G.**
Gor. 29/6—10/8/29.**G.**
Gor. 30/4—14/5/32.**G.**
Gor. 3—17/11/34.**G.**
Gor. 23/1—6/2/37.**G.**
Gor. 17/6—8/7/39.**G.**
Gor. 15/11—20/12/41.**G.**
Gor. 22—29/4/44.**H.**
Gor. 7—28/12/46.**G.**
New cylinders.
Gor. 2—9/10/48.**H.**

BOILERS:
335.
336 ?/1/07.
848 4/1/08.
1267 25/11/11.
478 30/6/17.
854 5/8/22.
592 *(superheated)* 1/11/24.
468 10/8/29.
891 14/5/32.
1634 17/11/34.
839 6/2/37.
830 8/7/39.
185 29/4/44.
3767 *(saturated)* 28/12/46.
913 9/10/48.

SHEDS:
Gorton 24/7/19.
Mexborough 16/2/24.
Colwick 1/1/31.
Langwith Jct. 9/1/31.
Retford 3/8/43.
Ardsley 5/10/47.

RENUMBERED:
6052 1/11/24.
3200 7/9/46.
63200 9/10/48.

CONDEMNED: 5/9/49.
Cut up at Gorton.

6053

Neilson Reid 6252.

To traffic 11/1902.

REPAIRS:
Gor. ?/?—15/12/06.**G.**
Gor. ?/?—20/3/09.**G.**
Gor. ?/?—31/1/14.**G.**
Gor. ?/?—19/4/19.**G.**
Gor. 18/6—13/8/21.**G.**
Gor. 17/11/23—12/4/24.**G.**
Gor. 26/6—4/9/26.**G.**
Gor. 27/10—24/11/28.**G.**
Gor. 29/8—3/10/31.**G.**
Gor. 12—19/1/35.**G.**
Gor. 10/7—7/8/37.**G.**

BOILERS:
336.
237 15/12/06.
1385 20/3/09.
1138 31/1/14.
1377 19/4/19.
468A 12/4/24.
911 *(superheated)* 24/11/28.
591 3/10/31.
595 19/1/35.
319 7/8/37.

SHEDS:
Mexborough.
Langwith Jct. 24/11/36
Barnsley 11/10/37.

RENUMBERED:
6053 12/4/24.

CONDEMNED: 28/2/39.
Cut up at Gorton.

6054

Neilson Reid 6253.

To traffic 11/1902.

REPAIRS:
Gor. ?/?—26/1/07.**G.**
Gor. ?/?—4/3/10.**G.**
Gor. ?/?—6/7/12.**G.**
Gor. ?/?—18/8/17.**G.**
Gor. 19/8/22—27/1/23.**G.**
Gor. 12/4—14/6/24.**G.**
Gor. 2/4—18/6/27.**G.**

Gor. 2/11—7/12/29.**G.**
Gor. 11—25/6/32.**G.**
Gor. 3—17/11/34.**G.**
Gor. 27/3—10/4/37.**G.**
Gor. 21/10—11/11/39.**G.**
Gor. 4—21/3/42.**G.**
New R.H. cylinder.
Gor. 17/3—8/4/44.**G.**
Gor. 27/1—17/2/45.**L.**
Gor. 27/7—17/8/46.**L.**
Gor. 26/4—10/5/47.**L.**
After collision.
Gor. 1—8/11/47.**H.**
Gor. 2—16/4/49.**G.**

BOILERS:
337.
214 26/1/07.
845 4/3/10.
1114 6/7/12.
846 18/8/17.
1401 *(superheated)* 27/1/23.
601 7/12/29.
896 25/6/32.
836 17/11/34.
896 10/4/37.
920 11/11/39.
185 21/3/42.
869 8/4/44.
3734 17/8/46.
852 8/11/47.
901 16/4/49.

SHEDS:
Mexborough 19/6/08.
Doncaster 30/1/30.
Mexborough 8/2/30.
Langwith Jct. 6/1/31.
Retford 3/8/43.
Grantham 28/9/46.
Barnsley 13/2/49.

RENUMBERED:
6054 14/6/24.
3201 17/8/46.
63201 14/4/49.

CONDEMNED: 22/1/51.
Into Gor. for cut up 27/1/51.

5056

Kitson 4202.

To traffic 9/1903.

REPAIRS:
Gor. ?/?—?/?/07.**G.**
Gor. ?/?—?/11/09.**G.**
Gor. ?/?—17/8/12.**G.**
Gor. ?/?—18/8/17.**G.**
Gor. 6/1—3/3/23.**G.**
Gor. 24/1—14/3/25.**G.**
Gor. 24/9—10/12/27.**G.**
New R.H. cylinder.
Gor. 21/6—26/7/30.**G.**
Gor. 15—22/10/32.**G.**
Gor. 15—22/12/34.**G.**
Gor. 26/6—3/7/37.**G.**
Gor. 27/4—18/5/40.**G.**
Gor. 9—28/8/43.**G.**
Gor. 16/3—20/4/46.**G.**
Gor. 27/11—18/12/48.**G.**

BOILERS:
837.
851 ?/?/07.
837 17/8/12.
1696 18/8/17.
1402 *(superheated)* 3/3/23.
841 10/12/27.
898 22/10/32.
829 22/12/34.
836 3/7/37.
1920 18/5/40.
374 *(saturated)* 28/8/43.
896 *(superheated)* 20/4/46.
875 18/12/48.

SHEDS:
Barnsley.
Sheffield 9/5/29.
Retford 3/6/29.
Barnsley 7/4/33.
Grantham 6/3/49.
Ardsley 4/6/50.

RENUMBERED:
5056 14/3/25.
3202 18/4/46.
63202 18/12/48.

CONDEMNED: 25/9/51.
Into Gor. for cut up 25/9/51.

5057

Kitson 4203.

To traffic 9/1903.

REPAIRS:
Gor. ?/?—22/5/09.**G.**

WORKS CODES:- Cw - Cowlairs. Dar- Darlington. Don - Doncaster. Ghd - Gateshead. Gor - Gorton. Inv - Inverurie. Str - Stratford.
REPAIR CODES:- **C/H** - Casual Heavy. **C/L** - Casual Light. **G** - General. **H**- Heavy. **H/I** - Heavy Intermediate. **L** - Light. **L/I** - Light Intermediate. **N/C** - Non-Classified.

Between February and April 1907 a further thirteen engines, Nos.1132 to 1144, were supplied by Kitson & Co. but these had 4000 gallons tenders. No.1144 was superheated from July 1915 and by Grouping Nos.133, 134, 139 and 143 were also superheated.

34

During February to December 1909, Gorton built fifteen, Nos.39, 44, 48, 49, 62, 63, 212, 213, 356 and 159 to 164, also with 4000 gallon tenders which had solid coal guards instead of four open rails used on previous tenders.

Another twenty engines, Nos.401, 1174 to 1177, 956 to 960, 1178, 1179, 961 to 965 and 1180 to 1182, were built at Gorton between June 1910 and February 1911. They were like the 1909 batch except that the splashers were now continuous over the three rear pairs of wheels.

Ex works 8th January 1916, No.1134 had been fitted with O4 type cylinders, 21in. diameter with 10in. piston valves instead of 19in. diameter and slide valves. It was also fitted with the Robinson Intensifore lubricating system. Superheating had started with No.57 in April 1914 and a Robinson steam circulating valve was fitted for element protection. The normal superheater was a Robinson 21-element type but from January 1916 to March 1924 No.1134 had twin headers and thirty-four ⅜in. diameter elements. Note large cover plates on smokebox for access to headers.

37

5057 cont./
Gor. ?/?—25/4/14.**G.**
Gor. ?/?—28/8/20.**G.**
Gor. 28/10/22—6/1/23.**G.**
Gor. 8/3—10/5/24.**G.**
Gor. 12/12/25—26/6/26.**G.**
Gor. 4/8—22/9/28.**G.**
New R.H. cylinder.
Gor. 23/8—27/9/30.**G.**
Gor. 11—25/2/33.**G.**
Gor. 19/10—2/11/35.**G.**
Gor. 7—21/5/38.**G.**
Gor. 17/8—7/9/40.**G.**
Gor. 19/3—1/5/43.**G.**
New L.H. cylinder.
Gor. 20/10—10/11/45.**G.**
Gor. 22/11—13/12/47.**G.**

BOILERS:
838.
861 22/5/09.
860 (superheated) 25/4/14.
1911 28/8/20.
722 26/6/26.
1632 27/9/30.
148 25/2/33.
875 2/11/35.
1682 21/5/38.
530 (saturated) 7/9/40.
894 1/5/43.
893 10/11/45.
3725 13/12/47.

SHEDS:
Mexborough 10/11/16.
Keadby *by* 1922.
Immingham 30/10/30.
Retford 9/8/43.
New England 12/12/43.
New England MGN 27/8/44.
Langwith Jct. 11/11/45.
Barnsley 7/4/46.
Langwith Jct. 27/10/46.
Barnsley 5/10/47.

RENUMBERED:
5057 10/5/24.
3203 18/8/46.

CONDEMNED: 6/11/50.
Into Gor. for cut up 11/11/50.

5058

Kitson 4204.

To traffic 10/1903.

REPAIRS:
Gor. ?/?—11/5/07.**G.**
Gor. ?/?—22/6/12.**G.**
Shipped to France 24/4/17.
Returned to U.K. 9/7/19.
Gor. 26/7—6/9/19.**G.**
New L.H. cylinder.

Gor. 16/4—4/6/21.**G.**
Gor. 31/3—22/9/23.**G.**
Gor. 12/12/25—27/2/26.**G.**
Gor. 1/12/28—26/1/29.**G.**
Gor. 20/12/30—17/1/31.**G.**
Gor. 27/5—17/6/33.**G.**
Gor. 22—29/2/36.**G.**
Gor. 4—11/3/39.**G.**
Gor. 30/11/40.**N/C.**
Boiler examination only.
Don. 24/1/42.
Rebuilt to Class Q1.

BOILERS:
839.
849 11/5/07.
1112 22/6/12.
1646 22/9/23.
589 (superheated) 26/1/29.
1677 17/1/31.
722 17/6/33.
835 29/2/36.
916 11/3/39.

SHEDS:
Mexborough.
Doncaster 19/5/25.
March 4/1/27.
Retford 28/2/29.
Barnsley 28/4/34.

RENUMBERED:
5058 27/2/26.

Tender sent to Gorton 4/4/42.

5059

Kitson 4205.

To traffic 10/1903.

REPAIRS:
Gor. ?/?—4/12/09.**G.**
Gor. ?/?—13/2/15.**G.**
New cylinders.
Gor. ?/?—25/12/20.**G.**
Gor. 6/1—17/2/23.**G.**
Gor. 14/2—23/5/25.**G.**
Gor. 19/11/27—21/1/28.**G.**
Gor. 29/9—20/10/28.**L.**
New R.H. cylinder.
Gor. 22/12/28—19/9/29.**L.**
New L.H. cylinder.
Gor. 16/8—27/9/30.**G.**
Gor. 18/6—9/7/32.**G.**
Gor. 26/5—9/6/34.**G.**
Gor. 6—20/2/37.**G.**
Gor. 7—21/10/39.**G.**
Don. 2—12/6/42.
To be photographed for Press
picture of a new O2 (3834)
with a secondhand tender to
save steel in wartime.
Gor. 9—23/1/43.**G.**

Gor. 27/10—17/11/45.**G.**
Gor. 23/10—6/11/48.**G.**
Tablet exchange apparatus
fitted at Grantham shed,
April 1949.

BOILERS:
840.
858 4/12/09.
1372 (superheated) 13/2/15.
1375 25/12/20.
894 21/1/28.
836 9/7/32.
643 9/6/34.
1916 20/2/37.
840 21/10/39.
19 (saturated) 23/1/43.
894 17/11/45.
3772 6/11/48.

SHEDS:
Barnsley.
Langwith Jct. 27/10/46.
Barnsley 5/10/47.
Grantham 13/2/49.
Ardsley 11/6/50.

RENUMBERED:
5059 23/5/25.
3204 18/8/46.
63204 6/11/48.

CONDEMNED: 25/6/51.
Cut up at Gorton.

5064

Kitson 4206.

To traffic 10/1903.

REPAIRS:
Gor. ?/?—19/10/07.**G.**
Gor. ?/?—5/2/10.**G.**
Gor. ?/?—17/7/15.**G.**
Gor. ?/?—14/8/20.**G.**
Gor. 5/8—7/10/22.**G.**
Gor. 14/6—15/11/24.**G.**
New R.H. cylinder.
Gor. 13/8—26/11/27.**G.**
Gor. 19/4—17/5/30.**G.**
Gor. 28/1—11/2/33.**G.**
Gor. 15—29/6/35.**G.**
Gor. 5—19/2/38.**G.**
Secondhand L.H. cylinder.
Gor. 31/8—12/10/40.**G.**
Gor. 4—15/5/43.**G.**
Gor. 25/8—15/9/45.**G.**
Gor. 6—27/12/47.**G.**

BOILERS:
841.
845 19/10/07.
869 5/2/10.
1410 (superheated) 17/7/15.

1373 14/8/20.
839 26/11/27.
1911 11/2/33.
915 29/6/35.
906 19/2/38.
138 12/10/40.
876 (saturated) 15/5/43.
913 15/9/45.
3771 27/12/47.

SHEDS:
Mexborough 14/12/03.
Sheffield 15/10/26.
Doncaster 15/12/26.
Mexborough ?/?
Annesley 5/1/31.
Ardsley 28/12/35.

RENUMBERED:
5064 15/11/24.
3205 15/9/46.

CONDEMNED: 26/12/50.
Into Gor. for cut up 30/12/50.

5065

Kitson 4207.

To traffic 10/1903.

REPAIRS:
Gor. ?/?—24/8/12.**G.**
Gor. ?/?—6/10/17.**G.**
Gor. 23/9—18/11/22.**G.**
Gor. 6/9—22/11/24.**G.**
Gor. 7/1—25/2/48.**G.**
New R.H. cylinder.
Gor. 22/3—12/4/30.**G.**
Gor. 24/9—8/10/32.**G.**
Gor. 2—16/3/35.**G.**
Gor. 7—14/8/37.**G.**
Gor. 30/12/39—13/1/40.**G.**
Gor. 4—18/1/41.**L.**
After derailment.
Gor. 15—29/11/41.**G.**
Gor. 21/2—11/3/44.**G.**
Gor. 21/12/46—1/2/47.**G.**

BOILERS:
842.
1265 24/8/12.
863 6/10/17.
1678 22/11/24.
530 12/4/30.
374 8/10/32.
328 16/3/35.
442 14/8/37.
54 13/1/40.
835 (superheated) 29/11/41.
891 11/3/44.

SHEDS:
Mexborough 14/3/10.
Doncaster 19/5/25.

From 1925 the protection of elements was provided automatically by a Gresley anti-vacuum valve behind the chimney. The latter had to be moved to a more forward position on superheated engines to clear the header.

Eight of the eighty-nine Q4's were never superheated and so kept the chimney in the central position on the smokebox top. These were Nos.5086, 5135, 5144, 5149, 5401, 6074 and 6075, withdrawn between 20th January 1936 and 6th January 1940, and No.6177 (3241 from 20th October 1946) not withdrawn until 17th April 1950.

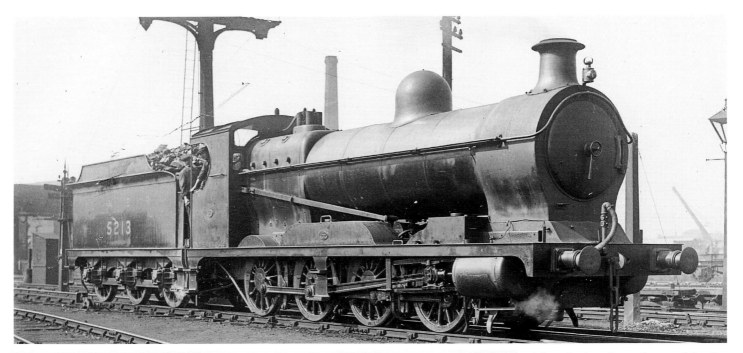

(above) **At Grouping, with the exception of one engine, this was the standard style for chimney and dome with whistle above the cab roof. Heights from rail level were: chimney 13ft 2¾in.; dome 13ft 4¾in.; whistle 13ft 2⁹⁄₁₆in.**

(left) **The exception was No.1176 which differed only in type of chimney. Ex works 2nd December 1922, it had the 'one-piece' chimney designed to obviate the taper type's proneness to cracking.**

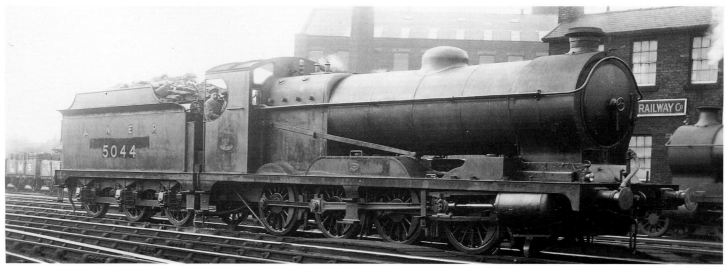

The LNER's decision to buy 125 ROD 2-8-0's meant that other work would have to be found for the 0-8-0's, possibly where the gauge was not so generous. In 1924/25 Gorton fitted at least eleven, Nos.5044, 5139, 5140, 5151, 5164, 5963, 6052, 6133, 6134, 6136 and 6178, with this 1ft 3in. plantpot chimney in conjunction with a new superheated boiler which had a low dome. Chimney height from rail level was then 12ft 4½in., dome 12ft 3¹⁄₁₆in., and whistle was moved to the firebox leaving a cab height at 12ft 7¹³⁄₁₆in. Note change to Ross 'pops' but not yet to Gresley anti-vacuum valve.

5065 cont./
March 15/7/25.
Sheffield 2/3/29.
Retford 16/3/29.
Grantham 28/9/46.

RENUMBERED:
5065 22/11/24.
3206 3/11/46.

CONDEMNED: 26/2/49.
Cut up at Gorton.

5067

Kitson 4208.

To traffic 10/1903.

REPAIRS:
Gor. ?/?—20/2/09.**G.**
Gor. ?/?—20/12/13.**G.**
Gor. ?/?—26/7/19.**G.**
Gor. 23/7—8/10/21.**G.**
Gor. 29/12/23—7/6/24.**G.**
Gor. 15/1—12/3/27.**G.**
Gor. 10/8—21/9/29.**G.**
Gor. 13—27/8/32.**G.**
New L.H. cylinder.
Gor. 19/1—2/2/35.**G.**
O4 chimney fitted.
Gor. 31/12/36—16/1/37.**G.**
Gor. 13—20/5/39.**G.**
Gor. 31/12/41—31/1/42.**G.**
Gor. 27/1—19/2/44.**G.**
New R.H. cylinder.
Gor. 14/12/46—4/1/47.**G.**
Gor. 19—26/3/49.**C/H.**
Gor. 3/6/50.**C/L.**

BOILERS:
843.
860 20/2/09.
855 20/12/13.
1138 26/7/19.
530 7/6/24.
525 *(superheated)* 21/9/29.
852 27/8/32.
839 2/2/35.
830 16/1/37.
851 20/5/39.
145 31/1/42.
3732 19/2/44.
3768 *(saturated)* 4/1/47.
3773 26/3/49.

SHEDS:
Mexborough 14/12/03.
Colwick 2/1/31.
Annesley 9/1/31.
Langwith Jct. 14/4/36.
Retford 3/8/43.
Grantham 28/9/46.
Ardsley 11/6/50.

RENUMBERED:
5067 7/6/24.
3207 17/10/46.
63207 26/3/49.

CONDEMNED: 7/8/50.
Into Gor. for cut up 12/8/50.

5068

Kitson 4209.

To traffic 11/1903.

REPAIRS:
Gor. ?/?—9/3/07.**G.**
Gor. ?/?—23/12/11.**G.**
Gor. ?/?—9/2/18.**G.**
Gor. 16/12/22—17/3/23.**G.**
Gor. 21/11—31/12/25.**G.**
Gor. 21/4—26/5/28.**G.**
Gor. 31/5—28/6/30.**G.**
Gor. 11—25/3/33.**G.**
Gor. 27/7—10/8/35.**G.**
Gor. 9—30/4/38.**G.**
Gor. 26/11—27/12/41.**G.**
Don. 21/6/44.
Rebuilt to Class Q1.

BOILERS:
844.
337 9/3/07.
1269 23/12/11.
1268 9/2/18.
1832 31/12/25.
418 26/5/28.
530 25/3/33.
418 10/8/35.
374 30/4/38.
3733 *(superheated)* 27/12/41.

SHED:
Barnsley.

RENUMBERED:
5068 31/12/25.
3208 *allocated.*

Tender sent to Gorton 5/8/44.

5070

Kitson 4210.

To traffic 11/1903.

REPAIRS:
Gor. ?/?—?/10/07.**G.**
Gor. ?/?—19/10/12.**G.**
Gor. ?/?—10/1/20.**G.**
Gor. 24/12/21—1/4/22.**G.**
Gor. 16/2—12/4/24.**G.**
Gor. 27/11/26—26/3/27.**G.**
Gor. 20/4—4/5/29.**G.**
New L.H. cylinder.

Gor. 25/10—29/11/30.**G.**
New R.H. cylinder.
Gor. 15—29/4/33.**G.**
Gor. 26/10—9/11/35.**G.**
Gor. 18—31/12/37.**G.**
Gor. 24/2—30/3/40.**G.**
Gor. 12/12/41—10/1/42.**G.**
Don. 6/9/43.
Rebuilt to Class Q1.

BOILERS:
845.
854 ?/10/07.
1268 19/10/12.
1829 10/1/20.
1817 26/3/27.
438 4/5/29.
1829 29/4/33.
876 *(superheated)* 9/11/35.
852 31/12/37.
643 10/1/42.

SHEDS:
Sheffield.
Barnsley 3/5/24.
Sheffield 8/1/30.
Retford 25/2/30.

RENUMBERED:
5070 12/4/24.
3209 *allocated.*

*Tender sent to Woodford
6/11/43 as water carrier.*

5071

Kitson 4211.

To traffic 11/1903.

REPAIRS:
Gor. ?/?—30/11/07.**G.**
Gor. ?/?—20/9/13.**G.**
Gor. ?/?—30/6/17.**G.**
Gor. 25/6—13/8/21.**G.**
Gor. 9/6—18/8/23.**G.**
Gor. 19/6—14/8/26.**G.**
Gor. 27/4—8/6/29.**G.**
Gor. 25/7—15/8/31.**G.**
Gor. 23/6—7/7/34.**G.**
Gor. 5/9—3/10/36.**G.**

BOILERS:
846.
855 30/11/07.
847 20/9/13.
1691 30/6/17.
1370 *(superheated)* 13/8/21.
591 8/6/29.
1842 15/8/31.
837 7/7/34.
647 3/10/36.

SHEDS:
Staveley.
Sheffield 29/6/29.
Barnsley 8/1/30.

RENUMBERED:
5071 14/8/26.

CONDEMNED: 7/6/39.
Cut up at Gorton.

5085

Kitson 4212.

To traffic 11/1903.

REPAIRS:
Gor. ?/?—11/1/08.**G.**
Gor. ?/?—21/1/11.**G.**
Gor. ?/?—7/2/14.**G.**
Gor. ?/?—24/5/19.**G.**
Gor. 25/6—8/10/21.**G.**
Gor. 24/11/23—5/4/24.**G.**
Gor. 21/8—30/10/26.**G.**
Gor. 22/9—3/11/28.**G.**
Gor. 5—26/10/29.**G.**
Gor. 9/4—14/5/32.**G.**
Secondhand R.H. cylinder.
Gor. 23/2—2/3/35.**G.**
Gor. 28/8—25/9/37.**G.**
New R.H. cylinder.
Gor. 17/2—6/4/40.**G.**
Gor. 11—23/5/42.**G.**
After collision.
Gor. 29/7—15/8/44.**G.**
Gor. 25/8—1/9/45.**L.**
Gor. 11/1—15/2/47.**G.**

BOILERS:
847.
841 11/1/08.
866 21/1/11.
1368 7/2/14.
1265 24/5/19.
438 5/4/24.
54 3/11/28.
374 26/10/29.
915 *(superheated)* 14/5/32.
1841 2/3/35.
847 25/9/37.
370 6/4/40.
642 23/5/42.
908 15/8/44.
3732 15/2/47.

SHEDS:
Mexborough 5/5/16.
Keadby *by* 10/22.
Immingham 29/10/29.
Keadby 11/6/32.
Frodingham 18/6/32.
Immingham 13/9/39.
Retford 9/8/43.
Ardsley 5/10/47.

5085 cont./
RENUMBERED:
5085 5/4/24.
3210 3/11/46.

CONDEMNED: 10/10/49.
Cut up at Gorton.

5086

Kitson 4213.

To traffic 11/1903.

REPAIRS:
Gor. ?/?—16/11/07.**G.**
Gor. ?/?—10/7/09.**G.**
Gor. ?/?—18/11/11.**G.**
Gor. ?/?—24/3/17.**G.**
Shipped to France 3/5/17.
Returned to UK 5/6/19.
Gor. 12/7—30/8/19.**G.**
Gor. 16/7—15/10/21.**G.**
Gor. 15/12/23—16/2/24.**G.**
Gor. 10/7—28/8/26.**G.**
Gor. 14/9—5/10/29.**G.**
Gor. 20—27/8/32.**G.**
Gor. 3—17/8/35.**G.**

BOILERS:
848.
862 16/11/07.
237 10/7/09.
841 18/11/11.
1678 24/3/17.
370 16/2/24.
1646 5/10/29.
1822 27/8/32.
530 17/8/35.

SHED:
Staveley.

RENUMBERED:
5086 16/2/24.

CONDEMNED: 10/4/37.
Cut up at Gorton.

5087

Kitson 4214.

To traffic 11/1903.

REPAIRS:
Gor. ?/?—2/2/07.**G.**
Gor. ?/?—15/8/08.**G.**
Gor. ?/?—6/8/10.**G.**
Gor. ?/?—28/6/13.**G.**
Gor. ?/?—15/5/15.**G.**
Gor. 12/6—24/7/20.**G.**
Gor. 29/4—24/6/22.**G.**
Gor. 31/1—28/3/25.**G.**
Gor. 11/12/26—28/5/27.**G.**

Gor. 2—30/11/29.**G.**
Gor. 1—15/10/32.**G.**
Gor. 16—30/11/35.**G.**
Gor. 31/7—28/8/37.**H.**
New R.H. cylinder.
Gor. 16—30/9/39.**G.**
Gor. 4—9/8/41.**H.**
Don. 14/3/44.
Rebuilt to Class Q1.

BOILERS:
849.
335 2/2/07.
336 15/8/08.
1266 6/8/10.
839 28/6/13.
1376 *(superheated)* 15/5/15.
1371 *(saturated)* 24/7/20.
1829 28/5/27.
1646 15/10/32.
1829 30/11/35.
838 *(superheated)* 30/9/39.
897 9/8/41.

SHED:
Barnsley.

RENUMBERED:
5087 28/3/25.
3211 allocated.

Tender to Gorton 14/4/44.

5091

Kitson 4215.

To traffic 11/1903.

REPAIRS:
Gor. ?/?—26/12/08.**G.**
Gor. ?/?—28/3/14.**G.**
Gor. ?/?—31/3/17.**G.**
Shipped to France 3/5/17.
Returned to UK 19/4/19.
Gor. 31/5—19/7/19.**G.**
Gor. 11/6—27/8/21.**G.**
Gor. 18/8/23—23/2/24.**G.**
Gor. 16/1—27/2/26.**G.**
Gor. 15/9—13/10/28.**G.**
Gor. 7—28/2/31.**G.**
Gor. 22/7—5/8/33.**G.**
Gor. 23—30/3/35.**G.**

BOILERS:
850.
844 26/12/08.
866 28/3/14.
1679 31/3/17.
906 *(superheated)* 13/10/28.
892 28/2/31.
907 5/8/33.
852 30/3/35.

SHED:
Barnsley.

RENUMBERED:
5091 23/2/24.

CONDEMNED: 17/11/37.
Cut up at Gorton.

5092

Kitson 4216.

To traffic 11/1903.

REPAIRS:
Gor. ?/?—9/2/07.**G.**
Gor. ?/?—23/4/10.**G.**
Gor. 3/7—25/9/20.**G.**
Gor. 20/1—17/3/23.**G.**
Gor. 19/9—21/11/25.**G.**
New cylinders.
Gor. 12/5—30/6/28.**G.**
Gor. 30/11—28/12/29.**G.**
Gor. 5—12/11/32.**G.**
Gor. 27/4—18/5/35.**G.**
Gor. 3—24/7/37.**G.**
Gor. 30/10—13/11/37.**L.**
Gor. 16—30/9/39.**G.**
Gor. 26/12/41—24/1/42.**G.**
Gor. 6—25/12/43.**G.**
New cylinders.
Gor. 14/9—5/10/46.**G.**

BOILERS:
851.
478 9/2/07.
1111 23/4/10.
1408 *(superheated)* 17/3/23.
901 30/6/28.
920 12/11/32.
319 18/5/35.
920 24/7/37.
185 30/9/39.
3734 24/1/42.
641 25/12/43.
3728 5/10/46.

SHEDS:
Gorton 30/8/21.
Staveley 2/2/24.
Barnsley 31/8/43.
Langwith Jct. 22/9/44.
Barnsley 7/4/46.

RENUMBERED:
5092 21/11/25.
3212 26/8/46.

CONDEMNED: 23/5/49.
Cut up at Gorton.

SHED:
Barnsley.

RENUMBERED:
5091 23/2/24.

CONDEMNED: 17/11/37.
Cut up at Gorton.

5135

Kitson 4217.

To traffic 1/1904.

REPAIRS:
Gor. ?/?—28/1/08.**G.**
Gor. ?/?—14/12/12.**G.**
Gor. ?/?—17/2/17.**G.**
Shipped to France 24/4/17.
Returned to UK 5/4/19.
Gor. ?/?—26/7/19.**G.**
Gor. 12/3—7/5/21.**G.**
Gor. 28/4—11/8/23.**G.**
Gor. 23/1—27/3/26.**G.**
Gor. 6/10—15/12/28.**G.**
Gor. 28/3—2/5/31.**G.**
Gor. 27/10—10/11/34.**G.**

BOILERS:
852.
857 28/1/08.
851 14/12/12.
336 17/2/17.
19 11/8/23.
328 15/12/28.
442 10/11/34.

SHEDS:
Mexborough.
Doncaster ?/?
March 31/1/27.
Ardsley 4/1/29.
Bradford 16/3/29.
Ardsley 23/4/34.

RENUMBERED:
5135 27/3/26.

CONDEMNED: 10/6/37.
Cut up at Gorton.

5136

Kitson 4218.

To traffic 1/1904.

REPAIRS:
Gor. ?/?—7/3/08.**G.**
Gor. ?/?—25/1/13.**G.**
Gor. ?/?—1/6/18.**G.**
Gor. 4/12/20—15/1/21.**G.**
Gor. 24/2—26/5/23.**G.**
Gor. 31/10—26/12/25.**G.**
Gor. 7/1—10/3/28.**G.**
New 21in. cylinders and
piston valves.
Gor. 25/4—16/5/31.**G.**
Gor. 27/1—10/2/34.**G.**
Gor. 17—31/10/36.**G.**
Gor. 5—19/8/39.**G.**
Gor. 11—29/11/41.**G.**
Gor. 28/2—18/3/44.**H.**

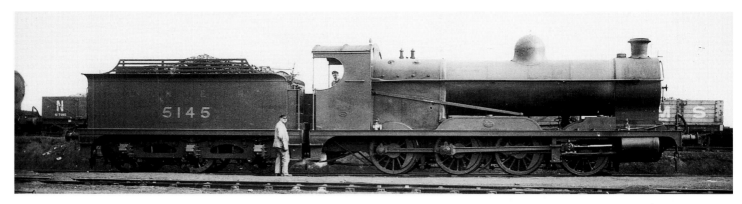

From January 1928 a plantpot chimney in alternative heights was introduced, 1ft 9in. high for superheated engines, giving height from rail of 12ft 10½in. But, as here, it was often paired with a pre-Grouping built boiler which did not have low dome. No.5145 got this 1920 built boiler ex works 29th November 1930, and thus remained outside LNER composite load gauge.

On the non-superheated engines the chimney was 2ft 1¼in. high, giving a height from rail of 13ft 2¾in. which was the same as original. The excess over the LNER 13ft 0in. posed no real problem, as off the GC they only moved to GN sheds, except for ten, Nos.5058, 5062, 5065, 5135, 5151, 5152, 5962, 5963, 6177, 6180 (only two of which were superheated), sent to March shed from July 1925 to March 1929 and from there they worked the Joint line to Doncaster which was to GN gauge.

Little real effort was thus made towards bringing this class within 13ft 0in. gauge. This non-superheated boiler built in March 1924 was altered to a low dome from 16th February 1929, but when used by No.5065 from 14th August 1937 to 30th December 1939, an original high dome cover was used, and whistle remained on top of cab.

No.5065 was not an isolated example. From 24th June 1933 to 11th May 1938 No.5152 had a 1914 built boiler with a dome of full height. This engine was not superheated until 8th February 1941 and then ran from 6th February 1943 to 30th December 1944 with another boiler from which the superheater had been taken out, but from 20th January 1945 it was again fitted with a superheater.

No.5152 became 3219 on 10th February 1946 by which date it had been fitted with a superheater for the second time. The war completely changed the attitude to this class; in January 1940 only forty-eight were left and they had been on the withdrawal list since November 1938. Scrapping was halted and from September 1939 those still with 2ft 1¼in. chimney were changed to 1ft 9in. type to bring them within 13ft 0in. gauge. Standard heights for all then became 12ft 10½in. at chimney, 12ft 3⅛in. at dome and 12ft 7¹³⁄₁₆in. at cab.

5136 cont./
New L.H. cylinder.
Gor. 12—26/5/45.**L.**
Gor. 7—28/6/47.**G.**

BOILERS:
853.
846 7/3/08.
1113 25/1/13.
1269 1/6/18.
1410 (superheated) 15/1/21.
1402 10/3/28.
912 16/5/31.
848 10/2/34.
838 31/10/36.
848 19/8/39.
869 29/11/41.
145 18/3/44.
915 28/6/47.

SHEDS:
Mexborough 1/4/04.
Doncaster 24/3/24.
Ardsley 5/6/28.

RENUMBERED:
5136 26/12/25.
3213 10/2/46.

CONDEMNED: 19/6/50.
Into Gor. for cut up 24/6/50.

5137

Kitson 4219.

To traffic 1/1904.

REPAIRS:
Gor. ?/?—?/7/05.**G.**
Gor. ?/?—?/?/08.**G.**
Gor. ?/?—8/2/13.**G.**
Gor. ?/?—4/5/18.**G.**
Gor. 14/10/22—24/2/23.**G.**
Gor. 8/8—26/9/25.**G.**
Gor. 25/2—21/4/28.**G.**
Gor. 10/5—21/6/30.**G.**
New L.H. cylinder.
Gor. 2—23/8/30.**L.**
New R.H. cylinder.
Gor. 6/12/30—24/1/31.**G.**
New 21in. cylinders and piston valves.
Gor. 25/3—1/4/33.**G.**
Gor. 30/3—6/4/35.**G.**
Gor. 7—21/11/36.**G.**
Gor. 14/5—4/6/38.**G.**
Gor. 21/12/40—11/1/41.**G.**
Gor. 27/9—9/10/43.**G.**
Gor. 28/9—23/11/46.**G.**

BOILERS:
854.
??? ?/7/05.
335 after 8/08.
857 8/2/13.
825 4/5/18.
1632 (superheated) 24/2/23.
1691 21/6/30.
319 1/4/33.
905 6/4/35.
910 21/11/36.
641 4/6/38.
906 9/10/43.
641 23/11/46.

SHEDS:
Barnsley.
Langwith Jct. 23/9/44.
Barnsley 7/4/46.

RENUMBERED:
5137 26/9/25.
3214 24/3/46.

CONDEMNED: 16/5/49.
Cut up at Gorton.

5138

Kitson 4220.

To traffic 2/1904.

REPAIRS:
Gor. ?/?—28/9/07.**G.**
Gor. ?/?—30/3/12.**G.**
Gor. ?/?—7/6/19.**G.**
Gor. 12/3—7/5/21.**G.**
Gor. 13/10—22/12/23.**G.**
Gor. 28/5—23/7/27.**G.**
Gor. 31/8—5/10/29.**G.**
Gor. 5—19/3/32.**G.**
Gor. 14—21/7/34.**G.**
Gor. 9—16/1/37.**G.**
Gor. 30/12/39—20/1/40.**G.**
Gor. 17/3—3/4/43.**G.**
Don. 30/6/45.
Rebuilt to Class Q1.

BOILERS:
855.
837 28/9/07.
337 30/3/12.
1364 7/6/19.
832 (superheated) 23/7/27.
47 19/3/32.
1916 21/7/34.
914 16/1/37.
3741 3/4/43.

SHEDS:
Staveley 17/2/22.
Barnsley 2/2/28.
Ardsley 10/10/29.

RENUMBERED:
5138 23/7/27.*
3215 *allocated.*
* *or earlier.*

Tender sent to Gorton 11/7/45.

5139

Kitson 4221.

To traffic 2/1904.

REPAIRS:
Gor. ?/?—3/8/07.**G.**
Gor. ?/?—20/5/11.**G.**
Gor. ?/?—24/2/17.**G.**
Shipped to France 1/5/17.
Returned to UK 10/5/19.
Gor. 21/6—26/7/19.**G.**
Gor. 18/9—13/11/20.**G.**
Gor. 17/3—9/6/23.**G.**
Gor. 27/6—24/10/25.**G.**
Gor. 3/3—14/4/28.**G.**
Gor. 22/6—27/7/29.**G.**
Gor. 14—28/12/29.**G.**
Gor. 5—19/3/32.**G.**
Gor. 2/8/34. *Not repaired.*

BOILERS:
856.
839 3/8/07.
1273 20/5/11.
1416 24/2/17.
1832 9/6/23.
641 (superheated) 24/10/25.
336 27/7/29.
915 28/12/29.
918 19/3/32.

SHEDS:
Keadby.
Immingham 10/1/30.
Keadby 11/6/32.
Frodingham 18/6/32.

RENUMBERED:
5139 24/10/25.

CONDEMNED: 18/8/34.
Cut up at Gorton.

5140

Kitson 4222.

To traffic 2/1904.

REPAIRS:
Gor. ?/?—7/12/07.**G.**
Gor. ?/?—13/1/12.**G.**
Gor. ?/?—14/4/17.**G.**
Shipped to France 16/5/17.
Returned to UK 16/7/19.
Gor. 26/7—23/8/19.**G.**
Gor. 27/11/20—15/1/21.**G.**
Gor. 24/2—30/6/23.**G.**
Gor. 13/6—10/10/25.**G.**
Gor. 4/2—17/3/28.**G.**
Gor. 9/3—13/4/29.**G.**
Gor. 21/2—14/3/31.**G.**
Gor. 20/5—3/6/33.**G.**
Gor. 7—21/12/35.**G.**

BOILERS:
857.
1114 7/12/07.
1272 13/1/12.
1677 14/4/17.
640 (superheated) 10/10/25.
552 13/4/29.
906 14/3/31.
832 3/6/33.
895 21/12/35.

SHEDS:
Keadby.
Frodingham 18/6/32.

RENUMBERED:
5140 10/10/25.

CONDEMNED: 27/11/37.
Cut up at Gorton.

5142

Kitson 4223.

To traffic 3/1904.

REPAIRS:
Gor. ?/?—28/3/08.**G.**
Gor. ?/?—28/9/12.**G.**
Gor. ?/?—24/11/17.**G.**
Gor. 2/12/22—24/2/23.**G.**
Gor. 21/2—27/6/25.**G.**
Gor. 24/12/27—11/2/28.**G.**
Gor. 25/5—29/6/29.**G.**
Gor. 7—21/2/31.**G.**
Gor. 4—18/11/33.**G.**
Gor. 12—26/10/35.**G.**
Gor. 13/11—4/12/37.**G.**

WORKS CODES:- Cw - Cowlairs. Dar- Darlington. Don - Doncaster. Ghd - Gateshead. Gor - Gorton. Inv - Inverurie. Str - Stratford.
REPAIR CODES:- C/H - Casual Heavy. C/L - Casual Light. G - General. H- Heavy. H/I - Heavy Intermediate. L - Light. L/I - Light Intermediate. N/C - Non-Classified.

45

5142 cont./
Gor. 10/2—2/3/40.**G.**
Gor. 11—16/5/42.**G.**
New cylinders.
Gor. 17/1—5/2/44.**G.**
Gor. 22/6—27/7/46.**G.**
Gor. 3—24/7/48.**G.**

BOILERS:
858.
847 28/3/08.
845 28/9/12.
1711 24/11/17.
1407 (superheated) 27/6/25.
640 29/6/29.
851 21/2/31.
892 18/11/33.
906 26/10/35.
908 4/12/37.
920 16/5/42.
3734 5/2/44.
201 (saturated) 27/7/46.
893 24/7/48.

SHEDS:
Barnsley.
Langwith Jct. 21/9/44.
Barnsley 7/4/46.
Langwith Jct. 27/10/46.
Barnsley 5/9/47.

RENUMBERED:
5142 27/6/25.
3216 26/1/46.
63216 24/7/48.

CONDEMNED: 5/9/49.
Cut up at Gorton.

5143

Kitson 4224.

To traffic 3/1904.

REPAIRS:
Gor. ?/?—10/12/10.**G.**
Gor. ?/?—31/5/19.**G.**
Gor. 12/3—30/4/21.**G.**
Gor. 14/7—15/12/23.**G.**
Gor. 20/2—17/4/26.**G.**
Gor. 30/6—28/7/28.**G.**
Gor. 2—30/11/29.**G.**
Gor. 19—26/11/32.**G.**
Gor. 15—29/12/34.**G.**
Gor. 10—31/7/37.**G.**

BOILERS:
859.
1264 10/12/10.
1403 31/5/19.
312 15/12/23.
431 28/7/28.
1902 30/11/29.
1918 (superheated) 26/11/32.

913 29/12/34.
370 31/7/37.

SHEDS:
Keadby.
Doncaster 3/12/29.
Barnsley 27/1/30.

RENUMBERED:
5143 17/4/26.

CONDEMNED: 17/11/39.
Into Gor. for cut up 18/11/39.

5144

Kitson 4225.

To traffic 3/1904.

REPAIRS:
Gor. ?/?—31/10/08.**G.**
Gor. ?/?—29/4/11.**G.**
Gor. 22/4—21/10/16.**G.**
Shipped to France 24/4/17.
Returned to UK 19/4/19.
Gor. 17/5—12/7/19.**G.**
Gor. 12/3—16/4/21.**G.**
Gor. 21/4—28/7/23.**G.**
Gor. 3/10—12/12/25.**G.**
Gor. 2—30/6/28.**G.**
Gor. 5/9—3/10/31.**G.**
Gor. 1—15/6/35.**G.**

BOILERS:
860.
865 31/10/08.
856 29/4/11.
1696 28/7/23.
522 30/6/28.
1817 3/10/31.
19 15/6/35.

SHEDS:
Immingham.
Ardsley 11/8/28.

RENUMBERED:
5144 12/12/25.

CONDEMNED: 14/5/38.
Cut up at Gorton.

5145

Kitson 4226.

To traffic 3/1904.

REPAIRS:
Gor. ?/?—?/?08.**G.**
Gor. ?/?—2/7/10.**G.**
Gor. ?/?—10/5/13.**G.**
Gor. ?/?—20/2/15.**G.**
Gor. 5/10—21/12/18.**G.**

Gor. 25/6—20/8/21.**G.**
Gor. 1/12/23—5/4/24.**G.**
Gor. 14/11—31/12/25.**G.**
Gor. 14/7—4/8/28.**G.**
Gor. 8—29/11/30.**G.**
Gor. 30/12/33—13/1/34.**G.**

BOILERS:
861.
868 ?/?/08.
1271 10/5/13.
929 (superheated) 20/2/15.
1378 (saturated) 21/12/18.
442 5/4/24.
1266 4/8/28.
1903 (superheated) 29/11/30.
838 13/1/34.

SHED:
Mexborough.

RENUMBERED:
5145 5/4/24.

CONDEMNED: 21/9/36.
Cut up at Gorton.

5146

Kitson 4227.

To traffic 3/1904.

REPAIRS:
Gor. ?/?—21/9/07.**G.**
Gor. ?/?—7/1/11.**G.**
Gor. ?/?—21/11/16.**G.**
Gor. 22/1—19/3/21.**G.**
New R.H. cylinder.
Gor. 7/7/23—17/5/24.**G.**
New L.H. cylinder.
Gor. 14/11—31/12/25.**G.**
Gor. 29/9—3/11/28.**G.**
Gor. 20/12/30—17/1/31.**G.**
Gor. 29/4—13/5/33.**G.**
Gor. 30/11—21/12/35.**G.**
Gor. 24/12/38—7/1/39.**G.**
Gor. 6/10—1/11/41.**G.**
Gor. 11—22/4/44.**G.**
Gor. 1—22/12/45.**G.**
Gor. 14/4—1/5/48.**G.**

BOILERS:
862.
856 21/9/07.
336 7/1/11.
1650 (superheated) 21/11/16.
1841 (saturated) 17/5/24.
1832 3/11/28.
550 17/1/31.
1902 13/5/33.
916 (superheated) 21/12/35.
1842 7/1/39.
3730 1/11/41.
835 22/4/44.

3722 22/12/45.
3735 1/5/48.

SHEDS:
Mexborough 21/12/12.
Sheffield 15/10/26.
Mexborough 8/12/26.
Ardsley 21/10/36.
Bradford 30/6/46.
Ardsley 4/6/50.

RENUMBERED:
5146 17/5/24.
3217 31/1/46.
63217 1/5/48.

CONDEMNED: 14/3/51.
Cut up at Gorton.

5147

Kitson 4228.

To traffic 3/1904.

REPAIRS:
Gor. ?/?—10/4/09.**G.**
New R.H. cylinder.
Gor. ?/?—5/9/14.**G.**
Gor. ?/?—18/8/17.**G.**
Gor. 27/5—18/11/22.**G.**
Gor. 16/8—25/10/24.**G.**
Gor. 1/1—25/6/27.**G.**
Gor. 17—28/9/29.**G.**
New L.H. cylinder.
Gor. 4/4—2/5/31.**G.**
Gor. 3—24/2/34.**G.**
Gor. 11/7—1/8/36.**G.**
Gor. 17—31/12/38.**G.**
Gor. 27/4—16/5/42.**G.**
Gor. 3—6/11/43.**L.**
Don. 28/10/44.
Rebuilt to Class Q1.

BOILERS:
863.
850 10/4/09.
1369 5/9/14.
1701 18/8/17.
1634 (superheated) 18/11/22.
643 2/5/31.
869 24/2/34.
851 1/8/36.
47 31/12/38.
851 16/5/42.

SHEDS:
Keadby.
Frodingham 18/6/32.
Bradford 27/8/39.
Ardsley 2/12/41.

RENUMBERED:
5147 25/10/24.
3218 allocated.

As late as November 1946 twelve new boilers were built and these were non-superheated. Nine were used on Q4 class and, after being spare from new in June 1948, two of the other three started work as stationery boilers in September/October 1950 whilst No.63234 had the other one from 16th April 1949 to its 5th March 1951 withdrawal, whence that boiler joined the stationery pool.

(above) **During the war it was decided that superheaters were not needed for Q4 class engines. No.5059 which had been superheated since February 1915 was ex works 23rd January 1943 with a July 1923 built saturated boiler which still had a tall dome cover. This put its height from rail level back to 13ft 3⅜in., duly recorded in Gorton's 'Special Fittings' register.**

(right) **Some boilers also had the superheater taken out. No.6133 (3224 from 29th August 1946) was ex works 20th June 1944 with a November 1929 built low-dome boiler from which the superheater had just been removed. Note that the chimney was moved back to the central position.**

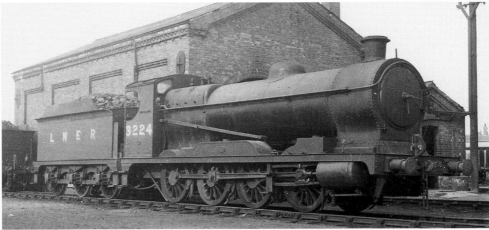

At least one fitted with a 1946-48 built boiler got a new dome cover of angular shape which Gorton had adopted during the war. No.63207 was so fitted from 26th March 1949. As No.5067 it was ex works 2nd February 1935 with an O4 class 1ft 5½in. chimney.

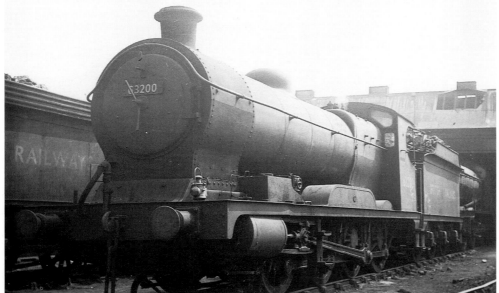

On these 1946-48 boilers the angular dome cover was only put on if a replacement was needed. Nos.63200 and 63234 continued to use round-top type covers.

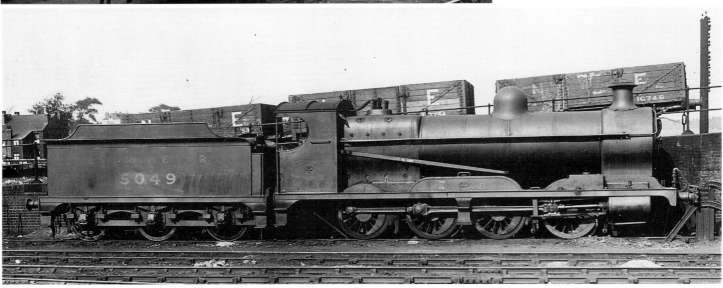

All originally were fitted with Ramsbottom safety valves, two on the first three engines but four on all the others. By Grouping only one boiler with two valves remained, and it was scrapped when No.135 went to works 28th April 1923. At first some had a rectangular casing enclosing the valves (*see* page 32, bottom) but these had gone by LNER take-over.

5147 cont./
Tender sent to Gorton 5/45.

5148

Kitson 4229.

To traffic 4/1904.

REPAIRS:
Gor. ?/?—23/4/10.**G**.
Gor. ?/?—11/3/16.**G**.
Gor. 29/1—16/4/21.**G**.
Gor. 28/4—20/10/23.**G**.
Gor. 17/10—19/12/25.**G**.
Gor. 5/1—2/3/29.**G**.
Gor. 20/6—1/8/31.**G**.
Gor. 30/9—7/10/33.**G**.
Gor. 15—19/2/36.**G**.

BOILERS:
864.
840 23/4/10.
1417 *(superheated)* 11/3/16.
1269 *(saturated)* 16/4/21.
129 20/10/23.
1679 2/3/29.
129 1/8/31.
550 7/10/33.
145 *(superheated)* 29/2/36.

SHEDS:
Mexborough.
Doncaster ?/4/29.
Ardsley 21/8/36.

RENUMBERED:
5148 19/12/25.

CONDEMNED: 29/10/38.
Cut up at Gorton.

5149

Kitson 4230.

To traffic 4/1904.

REPAIRS:
Gor. ?/?—23/6/08.**G**.
Gor. ?/?—4/9/09.**G**.
Gor. ?/?—10/11/17.**G**.
Gor. 27/5—29/7/22.**G**.
Gor. 29/3—6/9/24.**G**.
Gor. 8/1—5/3/27.**G**.
Gor. 13/7—10/8/29.**G**.
Gor. 31/10—21/11/31.**G**.
Gor. 17/2—10/3/34.**G**.
Gor. 6—27/6/36.**G**.

BOILERS:
865.
858 23/6/08.
863 4/9/09.
847 10/11/17.

1138 6/9/24.
19 10/8/29.
522 21/11/31.
129 10/3/34.
468A 27/6/36.

SHEDS:
Mexborough.
Sheffield 15/10/26.
Mexborough 7/12/26.
Barnsley 5/9/29.

RENUMBERED:
5149 6/9/24.

CONDEMNED: 9/12/39.
Into Gor. for cut up 16/12/39.

5150

Kitson 4231.

To traffic 4/1904.

REPAIRS:
Gor. ?/?—12/11/10.**G**.
Gor. ?/?—8/11/13.**G**.
Gor. 27/11/20—1/1/21.**G**.
Gor. 10/3—21/4/23.**G**.
Gor. 7/2—16/5/25.**G**.
Gor. 24/9—10/12/27.**G**.
Gor. 16/3—13/4/29.**G**.
Gor. 1—29/8/31.**G**.
Gor. 10—31/3/34.**G**.
Gor. 1—15/8/36.**G**.

BOILERS:
866.
1263 12/11/10.
1266 8/11/13.
1376 *(superheated)* 1/1/21.
842 10/12/27.
850 29/8/31.
419 31/3/34.
869 15/8/36.

SHEDS:
Keadby.
Frodingham 18/6/32.

RENUMBERED:
5150 16/5/25.

CONDEMNED: 6/3/39.
Cut up at Gorton.

5151

Kitson 4232.

To traffic 5/1904.

REPAIRS:
Gor. ?/?—?/?/09.**G**.
Gor. ?/?—2/11/12.**G**.

Gor. ?/?—14/8/15.**G**.
Gor. 6/11/20—1/1/21.**G**.
Gor. 24/2—12/5/23.**G**.
Gor. 10/10—12/12/25.**G**.
Gor. 1/12/28—12/1/29.**G**.
Gor. 9—30/5/31.**G**.
Gor. 7—21/4/34.**G**.
Gor. 26/9—10/10/36.**G**.

BOILERS:
867.
852 ?/?/09.
1404 *(superheated)* 14/8/15.
860 1/1/21.
647 12/12/25.
1402 30/5/31.
912 21/4/34.
837 10/10/36.

SHEDS:
Mexborough.
Doncaster ?/?
March 2/2/27.
Immingham 8/3/29.
Keadby 13/6/29.
Frodingham 18/6/32.

RENUMBERED:
5151 12/12/25.

CONDEMNED: 16/5/39.
Cut up at Gorton.

5152

Kitson 4233.

To traffic 5/1904.

REPAIRS:
Gor. ?/?—8/8/08.**G**.
Gor. ?/?—21/12/12.**G**.
Gor. ?/?—22/12/17.**G**.
Gor. 2/9/22—27/1/23.**G**.
Gor. 19/1—22/3/24.**G**.
Gor. 24/12/27—4/2/28.**G**.
Gor. 29/11—27/12/30.**G**.
Gor. 10—24/6/33.**G**.
Gor. 11—25/5/35.**G**.
Gor. 5/2—5/3/38.**G**.
Gor. 9/11/40—8/2/41.**G**.
Gor. 15/1—6/2/43.**G**.
New cylinders.
Gor. 30/12/44—20/1/45.**G**.
Gor. 1—8/6/46.**L**.
Gor. 14/12/46—18/1/47.**G**.

BOILERS:
868.
853 8/8/08.
854 21/12/12.
1367 22/12/17.
1411 27/1/23.
333 4/2/28.
468A 27/12/30.

1138 24/6/33.
374 25/5/35.
431 5/3/38.
876 *(superheated)* 8/2/41.
918 *(saturated)* 6/2/43.
851 *(superheated)* 20/1/45.
185 18/1/47.

SHEDS:
Mexborough 1/2/13.
Doncaster 2/4/24.
March 18/7/25.
Langwith Jct. 2/3/29.
Ardsley 28/2/34.
Barnsley 6/12/40.

RENUMBERED:
5152 22/3/24.
3219 10/2/46.

CONDEMNED: 26/12/49.
Into Gor. for cut up 31/12/49.

5153

Kitson 4234.

To traffic 5/1904.

REPAIRS:
Gor. ?/?—30/10/09.**G**.
Gor. ?/?—26/12/14.**G**.
Gor. ?/?—24/7/20.**G**.
Gor. 21/10—23/12/22.**G**.
Gor. 7/2—25/4/25.**G**.
Gor. 30/4—23/7/27.**G**.
Gor. 11/5—29/6/29.**G**.
Gor. 15/11—6/12/30.**G**.
Gor. 11/3—6/5/33.**G**.
New 21in. cylinders and
piston valves.
Gor. 28/12/35—18/1/36.**G**.
Gor. 4—25/6/38.**G**.
Gor. 11/1—1/2/41.**G**.
Gor. 8—22/5/43.**G**.
Gor. 17/1—9/2/46.**G**.
Gor. 18—25/5/46.**L**.
Gor. 6—20/11/48.**G**.

BOILERS:
869.
838 30/10/09.
862 *(superheated)* 26/12/14.
1406 24/7/20.
831 23/7/27.
165 6/12/30.
651 18/1/36.
3721 25/6/38.
650 22/5/43.
841 9/2/46.
3722 20/11/48.

SHEDS:
Keadby.
Frodingham 18/6/32.

5153 cont./
Barnsley 9/8/43.
Langwith Jct. 27/10/46.
Barnsley 5/10/47.

RENUMBERED:
5153 *25/4/25.*
3220 *9/2/46.*
63220 *20/11/48.*

CONDEMNED: 14/3/51.
Into Gor. for cut up 17/3/51.

6073

Kitson 4335.

To traffic 7/1905.

REPAIRS:
Gor. ?/?—9/3/12.**G.**
Gor. ?/?—7/4/17.**G.**
Shipped to France 16/5/17.
Returned to UK 20/6/19.
Gor. 19/7—23/8/19.**G.**
Gor. 6/8—8/10/21.**G.**
Gor. 15/9—22/12/23.**G.**
Gor. 29/1—16/7/27.**G.**
Superheater installed.
Gor. 28/12/29—1/2/30.**G.**
Gor. 17/9—1/10/32.**G.**

BOILERS:
1110.
 478 9/3/12.
1682 7/4/17.
 894 1/10/32.

SHEDS:
Mexborough.
Doncaster ?/?
Ardsley 15/10/27.
Keadby 16/10/29.
Ardsley 1/4/30.

RENUMBERED:
6073 *16/7/27 or earlier.*

CONDEMNED: 10/12/35.
Into Gor. for cut up 14/12/35.

6074

Kitson 4336.

To traffic 7/1905.

REPAIRS:
Gor. ?/?—2/10/09.**G.**
Gor. ?/?—1/8/14.**G.**
Gor. ?/?—2/10/20.**G.**
Gor. 14/10—25/11/22.**G.**
Gor. 5/1—29/3/24.**G.**
Gor. 19/6—14/8/26.**G.**

Instead of the rectangular casing enclosing all four valves, many had tubular casing to each valve. It is possible that No.5958 had Ramsbottom valves when it was withdrawn on 5th March 1937.

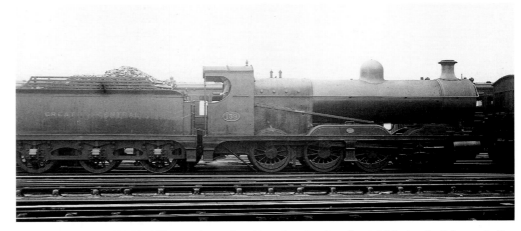

As early as May 1911 No.139 was changed to Ross 'pop' valves for trial but only this one boiler had them at Grouping. It was scrapped when No.1142 went in for repair on 7th July 1923.

Boilers built from June 1924 had Ross 'pops' as standard, and the 1924/27 batches had a shallow casing around the base of the valves.

6074 cont./
Gor. 18/8—29/9/28.**G.**
Gor. 30/8—4/10/30.**G.**
Gor. 24/6—8/7/33.**G.**

BOILERS:
1111.
  862 2/10/09.
1262 1/8/14.
1916 2/10/20.
1677 14/8/26.
  40 4/10/30.
438 8/7/33.

SHEDS:
Keadby.
Frodingham 18/6/32.

RENUMBERED:
6074 29/3/24.

CONDEMNED: 20/1/36.
Into Gor. for cut up 25/1/36.

6075

Kitson 4337.

To traffic 8/1905.

REPAIRS:
Gor. ?/?—14/5/10.**G.**
Gor. ?/?—7/10/16.**G.**
Shipped to France 17/4/17.
Returned to UK 10/5/19.
Gor. 28/6—2/8/19.**G.**
Gor. 19/2—19/3/21.**G.**
Gor. 28/4—10/11/23.**G.**
Gor. 6/3—24/4/26.**G.**
Gor. 17/11/28—16/2/29.**G.**
Gor. 14/11—5/12/31.**G.**
Gor. 19/1—2/2/35.**G.**
Gor. 4/9—2/10/37.**G.**

BOILERS:
1112.
  867 14/5/10.
1646 7/10/16.
  201 10/11/23.
  442 16/2/29.
   19 5/12/31.
  431 2/2/35.
  530 2/10/37.

SHEDS:
Mexborough 14/12/12.
Doncaster 15/12/23.
Mexborough 26/3/25.
Ardsley 5/3/29.

RENUMBERED:
6075 24/4/26.

CONDEMNED: 6/1/40.
Cut up at Gorton.

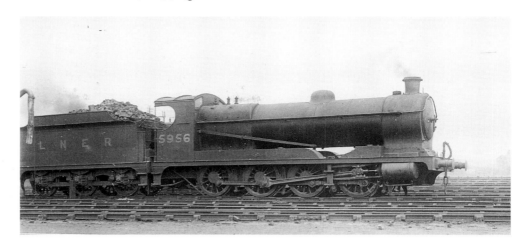

By 1929 the base casing was no longer fitted and was also discarded from earlier boilers.

Until after the height reduction began in 1924 all had the whistle mounted above the cab roof.

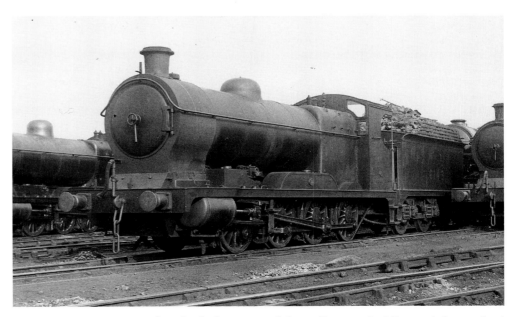

After the whistle was moved to the firebox, some of the earlier ones had it mounted on a short pipe.

6076

Kitson 4338.

To traffic 8/1905.

REPAIRS:
Gor. ?/?—24/12/10.**G.**
Gor. ?/?—28/4/17.**G.**
Shipped to France 30/5/17.
Returned to UK 5/6/19.
Gor. 12/7—23/8/19.**G.**
Gor. 7/5—6/8/21.**G.**
Gor. 24/2—14/4/23.**G.**
Gor. 2/5—4/7/25.**G.**
Gor. 13/8—29/10/27.**G.**
Gor. 1/2—8/3/30.**G.**
Gor. 23/5—4/7/31.**G.**
New 21in. cylinders and
piston valves.
Gor. 27/10—10/11/34.**G.**
Gor. 13—27/2/37.**G.**
Gor. 22/4—6/5/39.**G.**
Gor. 28/12/40.**L.**
Gor. 15/6—3/7/43.**H.**
New L.H. cylinder.
Gor. 28/7—18/8/45.**G.**
Gor. 9—30/3/46.**L.**
Secondhand L.H. cylinder.
Gor. 10—24/1/48.**G.**

BOILERS:
1113.
1110 24/12/10.
866 28/4/17.
1270 6/8/21.
1650 (*superheated*) 29/10/27.
1634 4/7/31.
370 10/11/34.
643 27/2/37.
911 6/5/39.
899 18/8/45.
905 24/1/48.

SHEDS:
Mexborough 8/11/19.
Keadby *by* 1922.
Ardsley 11/11/27.
Keadby 10/10/29.
Ardsley 22/3/30.

RENUMBERED:
6076 4/7/25.
3221 16/9/46.
ᴇ**3221** 24/1/48.

CONDEMNED: 26/12/50.
Into Gor. for cut up 30/12/50.

6077

Kitson 4339.

To traffic 8/1905.

REPAIRS:
Gor. ?/?—4/1/08.**G.**
Gor. ?/?—12/8/09.**G.**
Gor. ?/?—8/4/16.**G.**
Gor. 11/3—6/5/22.**G.**
Gor. 11/8—20/10/23.**G.**
Gor. 21/2—18/4/25.**G.**
Gor. 19/11/27—4/2/28.**G.**
Gor. 22/3—26/4/30.**G.**
Gor. 8—15/10/32.**G.**
Gor. 8—22/12/34.**G.**
Gor. 6—13/2/37.**G.**
Gor. 26/10—30/11/40.**G.**
Don. 1/10/43.
Rebuilt to Class Q1.

BOILERS:
1114.
852 4/1/08.
843 12/8/09.
1610 (*superheated*) 8/4/16.
1415 6/5/22.
897 4/2/28.
723 15/10/32.
650 22/12/34.
891 13/2/37.
431 (*saturated*) 30/11/40.

SHEDS:
Langwith Jct. 20/6/14.
Mexborough 5/6/37.

RENUMBERED:
6077 18/4/25.
3222 allocated.

Tender sent to Woodford as
a water carrier 6/11/43.

6132

Kitson 4475.

To traffic 2/1907.

REPAIRS:
Gor. ?/?—28/3/14.**G.**
Gor. ?/?—24/1/20.**G.**
Gor. 12/11/21—14/1/22.**G.**
Gor. 24/2—7/4/23.**G.**
Gor. 10/5—5/7/24.**G.**
Gor. 21/11/25—23/1/26.**G.**
Gor. 21/1—3/3/28.**G.**
Gor. 9—23/6/28.**L.**
New cylinders.

Gor. 28/6—2/8/30.**G.**
Gor. 14—28/1/33.**G.**
Gor. 20—27/7/35.**G.**
Gor. 5—12/2/38.**G.**
Gor. 28/9—26/10/40.**G.**
Gor. 7—28/11/42.**G.**
Gor. 7—21/4/45.**G.**
Gor. 21—28/7/45.**L.**
Gor. 13/3—10/4/48.**G.**

BOILERS:
1262.
195 28/3/14.
1832 24/1/20.
418 7/4/23.
319 (*superheated*) 3/3/28.
1678 28/1/33.
525 27/7/35.
138 12/2/38.
728 26/10/40.
832 28/11/42.
3735 21/4/45.
3741 10/4/48.

SHEDS:
Langwith Jct. 9/4/20.
Colwick 21/2/34.
Ardsley 7/10/35.

RENUMBERED:
6132 5/7/24.
3223 6/10/46.
63223 10/4/48.

CONDEMNED: 11/6/51.
Into Gor. for cut up 16/6/51.

6133

Kitson 4476.

To traffic 2/1907.

REPAIRS:
Gor. ?/?—24/9/10.**G.**
Gor. ?/?—3/10/14.**G.**
Gor. ?/?—20/4/18.**G.**
Gor. 25/3—20/5/22.**G.**
Gor. 23/2—3/5/24.**G.**
Gor. 23/1—10/7/26.**G.**
Gor. 24/3—28/4/28.**G.**
Gor. 12/4—10/5/30.**G.**
Gor. 5—19/3/32.**G.**
Gor. 1—22/9/34.**G.**
Gor. 30/1—13/2/37.**G.**
Gor. 6—20/1/40.**G.**
Gor. 24/7—22/8/42.**G.**
New cylinders.
Gor. 10—20/6/44.**H.**
Gor. 19/10—9/11/46.**G.**

BOILERS:
1263.
1274 24/9/10.
1377 3/10/14.
854 20/4/18.
1413 (*superheated*) 20/5/22.
723 10/7/26.
650 10/5/30.
553 19/3/32.
1920 22/9/34.
1901 13/2/37.
896 20/1/40.
908 22/8/42.
920 (*saturated*) 20/6/44.

SHEDS:
Langwith Jct. 7/11/14.
Retford 3/8/43.
Ardsley 5/10/47.

RENUMBERED:
6133 3/5/24.
3224 29/8/46.

CONDEMNED: 26/2/49.
Cut up at Gorton.

6134

Kitson 4477.

To traffic 2/1907.

REPAIRS:
Gor. ?/?—23/7/10.**G.**
Gor. ?/?—9/3/12.**G.**
Gor. 27/3/15—8/1/16.**G.**
New 21in. cylinders and
piston valves.
Gor. 26/11/21—11/3/22.**G.**
Gor. 22/3—4/10/24.**G.**
Gor. 19/12/25—13/2/26.**G.**
Gor. 19/5—7/7/28.**G.**
Gor. 11/10—1/11/30.**G.**
Gor. 26/11—17/12/32.**G.**
Gor. 19/1—9/2/35.**G.**
Gor. 20/3—10/4/37.**G.**
Gor. 22/7—12/8/39.**G.**
Gor. 5—19/4/41.**G.**
Gor. 5—30/8/41.**G.**
Gor. 8—26/6/43.**G.**
Gor. 30/6/45. *Tender only.*
Gor. 9/3—6/4/46.**G.**
Gor. 16/10—6/11/48.**G.**

BOILERS:
1264.
1112 23/7/10.
237 9/3/12.
865 (*superheated*) 8/1/16.
589 4/10/24.

WORKS CODES:- Cw - Cowlairs. Dar- Darlington. Don - Doncaster. Ghd - Gateshead. Gor - Gorton. Inv - Inverurie. Str - Stratford.
REPAIR CODES:- **C/H** - Casual Heavy. **C/L** - Casual Light. **G** - General. **H**- Heavy. **H/I** - Heavy Intermediate. **L** - Light. **L/I** - Light Intermediate. **N/C** - Non-Classified.

52

By 1928 the standard position was closer to the firebox crown plate and the whistle was little taller than the safety valves.

Until 1947, smokebox door fastening was by wheel and handle. Note load class 6 collar on standpipe.

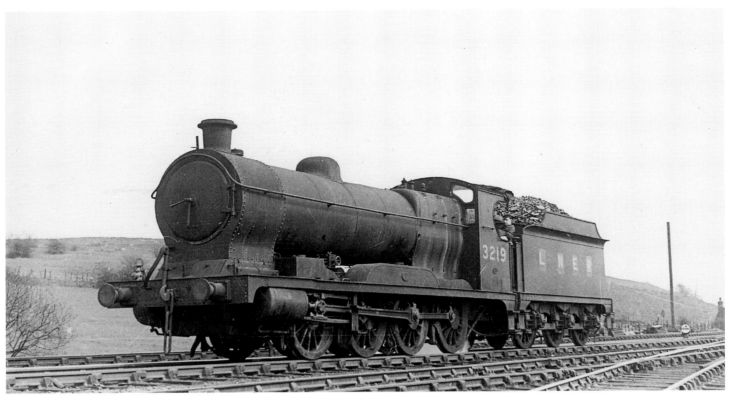

No.3219 ex works 18th January 1947 had its wheel replaced by another handle and others were dealt with similarly at subsequent shoppings.

The upper lamp iron was above the smokebox and until October 1948 remained there, so that a few of the last survivors still had it in that position at withdrawal. No.63217 was last ex works 1st May 1948 and was withdrawn 14th March 1951, as shown in this 15th April 1951 photograph.

Beginning with No.63200, ex works 9th October 1948, the upper lamp iron was moved on to the smokebox door to improve access and reduce risk from overhead electrification wiring on the Manchester to Sheffield and Wath routes over Woodhead. On only twelve was this move made, Nos.63200, 63201, 63202, 63204, 63207, 63220, 63225, 63227, 63233, 63234, 63240 and 63243, No.63243 being the last on 23rd April 1949 although No.63201 is here running trials following a general repair, including boiler change, on 16th April 1949. It was clearly not repainted.

6134 cont./
1903 7/7/28.
835 1/11/30.
841 17/12/32.
646 9/2/35.
905 12/8/39.
3726 26/6/43.
3742 6/11/48.

SHEDS:
Gorton 4/2/16.
Langwith Jct. 9/2/24.
Retford 3/8/43.
New England 12/12/43.
New England MGN 27/8/44.
Retford 28/10/45.
Grantham 1/9/46.
Ardsley 22/4/47.

RENUMBERED:
6134 4/10/24.
3225 8/10/46.
63225 6/11/48.

CONDEMNED: 25/9/51.
Cut up at Gorton.

6135

Kitson 4478.

To traffic 3/1907.

REPAIRS:
Gor. ?/?—24/2/12.**G.**
Gor. ?/?—9/6/17.**G.**
Gor. ?/?—18/10/19.**G.**
Gor. 18/6—17/9/21.**G.**
Gor. 10/3—5/5/23.**G.**
Gor. 20/12/24—31/1/25.**G.**
Gor. 22/1—4/6/27.**G.**
Gor. 16/2—16/3/29.**G.**
Gor. 11—25/4/31.**G.**
Gor. 14/1—4/2/33.**G.**
New R.H. cylinder.
Gor. 1—15/2/36.**G.**
Gor. 28/1—11/2/39.**G.**
Gor. 15/4/39.**L.**
Slide valves re-faced.
Gor. 15/3—5/4/41.**G.**
Gor. 21/7—7/8/43.**G.**
Gor. 15/9—6/10/45.**G.**
Gor. 25/1/47.**L.**
Firehole ring fractured.
Gor. 6/10/47—10/1/48.**G.**

BOILERS:
1265.
848 24/2/12.
1272 9/6/17.
1407 *(superheated)* 18/10/19.
1817 *(saturated)* 31/1/25.
352 4/6/27.
312 25/4/31.
145 *(superheated)* 4/2/33.

1772 15/2/36.
3725 11/2/39.
495 5/4/41.
893 *(saturated)* 7/8/43.
876 6/10/45.
3770 10/1/48.

SHEDS:
Langwith Jct..
Ardsley 7/5/31.

RENUMBERED:
6135 31/1/25.
3226 6/10/46.

CONDEMNED: 16/10/50.
Into Gor. for cut up 21/10/50.

6136

Kitson 4479.

To traffic 3/1907.

REPAIRS:
Gor. ?/?—18/6/10.**G.**
Gor. ?/?—1/5/15.**G.**
Gor. ?/?—22/3/19.**G.**
Gor. 19/3—30/4/21.**G.**
Gor. 26/5—17/11/23.**G.**
Gor. 7/3—25/4/25.**G.**
Gor. 26/3—14/5/27.**G.**
Gor. 28/9—26/10/29.**G.**
Gor. 31/12/31—16/1/32.**G.**
Gor. 9—30/6/34.**G.**
Gor. 13—27/6/36.**G.**
Gor. 20/8—3/9/38.**G.**
Gor. 11/1—8/3/41.**G.**
Gor. 7—24/7/43.**G.**
Gor. 9/3—6/4/46.**G.**
Gor. 23/10—13/11/48.**G.**

BOILERS:
1266.
864 18/6/10.
1407 *(superheated)* 1/5/15.
1113 *(saturated)* 22/3/19.
601 *(superheated)* 25/4/25.
553 26/10/29.
842 16/1/32.
850 30/6/34.
553 27/6/36.
876 3/9/38.
722 8/3/41.
914 *(saturated)* 24/7/43.
3767 13/11/48.

SHEDS:
Langwith Jct. 1/9/22.
Retford 3/8/43.
New England 12/12/43.
New England MGN 27/8/44.
Langwith Jct. 28/10/45.
Barnsley 14/4/46.
Langwith Jct. 27/10/46.

Barnsley 5/10/47.
Ardsley 8/50.

RENUMBERED:
6136 25/4/25.
3227 3/11/46.
63227 13/11/48.

CONDEMNED: 26/5/51.
Cut up at Gorton.

6137

Kitson 4480.

To traffic 3/1907.

REPAIRS:
Gor. ?/?—26/8/11.**G.**
Gor. ?/?—26/4/13.**G.**
Gor. ?/?—4/8/17.**G.**
Gor. 2/9/22—27/1/23.**G.**
Gor. 29/3—17/5/24.**G.**
Gor. 1/5—17/6/26.**G.**
Gor. 16/6—14/7/28.**G.**
Gor. 19/7—23/8/30.**G.**
Gor. 17/9—1/10/32.**G.**
Gor. 12—26/1/35.**G.**
Gor. 25/9—9/10/37.**G.**

BOILERS:
1267.
1271 26/8/11.
846 26/4/13.
1110 4/8/17.
1267 27/1/23.
1266 17/6/26.
1901 *(superheated)* 14/7/28.
723 23/8/30.
525 1/10/32.
898 26/1/35.
918 9/10/37.

SHEDS:
Langwith Jct..
Colwick 23/2/34.
Ardsley 2/11/35.

RENUMBERED:
6137 17/5/24.

CONDEMNED: 28/2/39.
Cut up at Gorton.

6138

Kitson 4481.

To traffic 3/1907.

REPAIRS:
Gor. ?/?—13/7/12.**G.**
Gor. ?/?—8/4/16.**G.**
Gor. 27/12/19—21/2/20.**G.**
Gor. 4/3—20/5/22.**G.**

Gor. 15/12/23—10/5/24.**G.**
Gor. 21/11/25—9/1/26.**G.**
Gor. 18/2—12/5/28.**G.**
Gor. 26/4—24/5/30.**G.**
Gor. 22/10—5/11/32.**G.**

BOILERS:
1268.
849 13/7/12.
1406 *(superheated)* 8/4/16.
1841 *(saturated)* 21/2/20.
522 10/5/24.
849 *(superheated)* 12/5/28.
646 5/11/32.

SHEDS:
Langwith Jct..
Colwick 20/2/34.

RENUMBERED:
6138 10/5/24.

CONDEMNED: 5/12/34.
Into Gor. for cut up 8/12/34.

6139

Kitson 4482.

To traffic 3/1907.

REPAIRS:
Gor. ?/?—23/9/11.**G.**
Gor. ?/?—25/9/15.**G.**
Gor. 15/4—25/11/22.**G.**
Gor. 23/2—3/5/24.**G.**
Gor. 17/4—10/7/26.**G.**
Gor. 19/11/27—28/1/28.**G.**
Gor. 25/1—15/2/30.**G.**
Gor. 19—31/12/31.**G.**
Gor. 18/8—15/9/34.**G.**
Gor. 15—29/8/36.**G.**
Gor. 9—30/1/37.**L.**
Gor. 28/8—4/9/37.**L.**
Gor. 10—24/12/38.**G.**
Gor. 25/5—15/6/40.**G.**
New R.H. cylinder.
Don. 27/10/42.
Rebuilt to Class Q1.

BOILERS:
1269.
865 23/9/11.
858 *(superheated)* 25/9/15.
1412 25/11/22.
896 28/1/28.
419 15/2/30.
1920 31/12/31.
1701 15/9/34.
3724 29/8/36.
849 24/12/38.
836 15/6/40.

SHED:
Langwith Jct.

Between late 1946 and the end of May 1950, eleven Nos.3201, 3202, 3204, 3206, 3207, 3225, 3228, 3229, 3234, 3240 and 3243, when stationed at Grantham worked iron ore trains on the High Dyke branch and for this were equipped with tablet exchanging apparatus.

The last six Q4 at Grantham left in two batches during 1950; Nos.63202, 63234 and 63240 on 4th June, and Nos.63204, 63207 and 63243 on the 11th June. Note they had tablet apparatus on both sides, but this was then removed by Ardsley shed.

6139 cont./
RENUMBERED:
6139 3/5/24.

Tender sent to Gorton 1/1/43.

6140

Kitson 4483.

To traffic 3/1907.

REPAIRS:
Gor. ?/?—17/1/14.**G.**
Gor. ?/?—25/8/17.**G.**
Gor. 12/8—2/12/22.**G.**
Gor. 23/2—19/4/24.**G.**
Gor. 16/10/26—15/1/27.**G.**
New cylinders.
Gor. 15/6—13/7/29.**G.**
Gor. 11/4—2/5/31.**G.**
Gor. 1—29/4/33.**G.**
Gor. 9—23/5/36.**G.**
Gor. 3/9—8/10/38.**G.**
Gor. 14—28/12/40.**G.**
Gor. 19/8—5/9/42.**G.**
After collision.
Gor. 3—21/10/44.**G.**
Gor. 21/6—2/8/47.**G.**

BOILERS:
1270.
1367 17/1/14.
1114 25/8/17.
1701 2/12/22.
 374 15/1/27.
 201 13/7/29.
 651 *(superheated)* 2/5/31.
1691 29/4/33.
 849 23/5/36.
 915 8/10/38.
3737 5/9/42.
 642 21/10/44.
 145 2/8/47.

SHEDS:
Langwith Jct. 20/6/12.
Colwick 26/1/27.
Keadby 11/9/29.
Immingham 25/3/31.
Colwick 4/10/41.
Langwith Jct. 5/10/41.
Immingham 16/10/41.
Lincoln 7/5/42.
Retford 12/12/43.
New England 27/5/45.
Retford 28/10/45.
Grantham 28/9/46.

RENUMBERED:
6140 19/4/24.
3228 30/11/46.

CONDEMNED: 15/8/49.
Cut up at Gorton.

6141

Kitson 4484.

To traffic 3/1907.

REPAIRS:
Gor. ?/?—11/3/11.**G.**
Gor. ?/?—3/2/17.**G.**
Shipped to France 17/4/17.
Returned to UK 5/6/19.
Gor. 12/7—9/8/19.**G.**
Gor. 30/7—1/10/21.**G.**
Gor. 25/8—22/3/24.**G.**
Gor. 21/11/25—13/2/26.**G.**
Gor. 18/2—28/4/28.**G.**
Gor. 5/4—17/5/30.**G.**
Gor. 20/2—5/3/32.**G.**
Gor. 4—18/8/34.**G.**
Gor. 31/10—14/11/36.**G.**
Don. 23—25/11/38.**N/C.**

BOILERS:
1271.
 859 11/3/11.
 431 22/3/24.
 847 *(superheated)* 28/4/28.
1701 5/3/32.
1903 18/8/34.
 848 14/11/36.

SHED:
Langwith Jct.

RENUMBERED:
6141 22/3/24.

CONDEMNED: 31/1/39.
Cut up at Gorton.

6142

Kitson 4485.

To traffic 3/1907.

REPAIRS:
Gor. ?/?—21/10/11.**G.**
Gor. ?/?—5/7/13.**G.**
Gor. ?/?—20/1/17.**G.**
Shipped to France 24/4/17.
Returned to UK 8/6/19.
Gor. 12/7—2/8/19.**G.**
Gor. 30/7—8/10/21.**G.**
Gor. 7/7—1/12/23.**G.**
Gor. 17/1—7/3/25.**G.**
Gor. 18/6—3/9/27.**G.**
Gor. 16/6—21/7/28.**G.**
Gor. 9/8—6/9/30.**G.**
Gor. 31/12/32—14/1/33.**G.**
Gor. 4—18/5/35.**G.**

BOILERS:
1272.
 839 21/10/11.

 335 5/7/13.
1273 20/1/17.
1650 *(superheated)* 1/12/23.
 835 3/9/27.
1901 6/9/30.
 903 14/1/33.
 138 18/5/35.

SHED:
Langwith Jct.

RENUMBERED:
6142 7/3/25.

CONDEMNED: 22/5/37.
Cut up at Gorton.

6143

Kitson 4486.

To traffic 4/1907.

REPAIRS:
Gor. ?/?—25/2/11.**G.**
Gor. ?/?—23/11/12.**G.**
Gor. ?/?—2/3/18.**G.**
Gor. 1/10/21—7/1/22.**G.**
Gor. 2/6—1/9/23.**G.**
Gor. 20/12/24—14/2/25.**G.**
Gor. 19/11/27—7/1/28.**G.**
Gor. 24/1—14/2/31.**G.**
Gor. 14—21/10/33.**G.**

BOILERS:
1273.
1113 25/2/11.
 842 23/11/12.
 845 2/3/18.
 869 *(superheated)* 7/1/22.
 892 7/1/28.
 831 14/2/31.
 647 21/10/33.

SHEDS:
Langwith Jct.
Ardsley 31/1/28.

RENUMBERED:
6143 14/2/25.

CONDEMNED: 16/5/36.
Cut up at Gorton.

6144

Kitson 4487.

To traffic 4/1907.

REPAIRS:
Gor. ?/?—10/7/15.**G.**
Gor. ?/?—25/9/20.**G.**
Gor. 11/11/22—13/1/23.**G.**
Gor. 8/3—3/5/24.**G.**

Gor. 16/10/26—26/2/27.**G.**
Gor. 20/10—1/12/28.**G.**
Gor. 5/7—2/8/30.**G.**
Gor. 24/12/32—7/1/33.**G.**
Gor. 14—31/12/35.**G.**

BOILERS:
1274.
1370 *(superheated)* 10/7/15.
1263 25/9/20.
1911 26/2/27.
1678 2/8/30.
 835 7/1/33.
 728 31/12/35.

SHEDS:
Keadby.
Immingham 2/8/30.

RENUMBERED:
6144 3/5/24.

CONDEMNED: 7/1/38.
Cut up at Gorton.

5039

Gorton.

To traffic 2/1909.

REPAIRS:
Gor. ?/?—31/1/14.**G.**
Gor. ?/?—31/7/20.**G.**
Gor. 15/7—16/9/22.**G.**
Gor. 3/5—23/8/24.**G.**
Gor. 18/6—6/8/27.**G.**
Gor. 10/8—21/9/29.**G.**
Gor. 4—11/6/32.**G.**
Gor. 22/12/34—12/1/35.**G.**
Gor. 3—17/7/37.**G.**
Gor. 24/8—28/9/40.**G.**
Gor. 21/8—4/9/43.**G.**
Gor. 7—28/6/47.**G.**
Gor. 20—27/12/47.**H.**

BOILERS:
1364.
1263 31/1/14.
1902 31/7/20.
 834 *(superheated)* 6/8/27.
 905 11/6/32.
 333 12/1/35.
 829 17/7/37.
 906 28/9/40.
 495 4/9/43.
3737 28/6/47.
3736 27/12/47.

SHEDS:
Keadby.
Frodingham 18/6/32.
Barnsley 7/1/39.
Mexborough 7/12/39.
Grantham 23/2/47.

Taper-shank buffers were only fitted on the first three engines and No.6052 still had them in 1935, although by then they had been changed to GCR type on Nos.6053 and 6054. No.6052 had the same change later.

This was the standard pattern of GCR coupling hook and parallel shank buffers with end collar normally used by the class.

Some had GC coupling hook replaced by Group Standard type which had a square flange fixing to the buffer beam. To compensate for its extra length, substantial wood packing was placed between buffer flanges and buffer beam.

Whilst still fitted with Great Central type drawhook and buffer shanks, at least one had oval head buffers fitted. No.63202 (*see* page 57, bottom) also had oval heads whilst No.3229 had one oval and one circular buffer head (*see* page 76, top). Note rear sandbox has outside filler; only Nos.5064 and 6179 so noted.

5039 cont./
Barnsley 6/3/49.

RENUMBERED:
5039 23/8/24.
3229 14/7/46.

CONDEMNED: 4/12/50.
Cut up at Gorton.

5044

Gorton.

To traffic 4/1909.

REPAIRS:
Gor. ?/?—2/5/14.**G.**
Gor. ?/?—29/9/17.**G.**
Gor. 3/12/21—4/2/22.**G.**
Gor. 8/3—26/7/24.**G.**
Gor. 24/4—17/7/26.**G.**
Gor. 10/11/28—5/1/29.**G.**
Gor. 11/4—9/5/31.**G.**
Gor. 15/12/34—5/1/35.**G.**
Gor. 10/7—14/8/37.**G.**
New R.H. cylinder.
Gor. 18/3—1/4/39.**G.**
Gor. 27/10—15/11/41.**G.**
Don. 24/11/43.
Rebuilt to Class Q1.

BOILERS:
1365.
1364 *(ex5039)* 2/5/14.
  837 29/9/17.
  845 4/2/22.
  552 *(superheated)* 26/7/24.
  912 5/1/29.
  595 9/5/31.
  847 5/1/35.
  595 14/8/37.
  835 1/4/39.
3732 15/11/41.

SHEDS:
Mexborough.
Langwith Jct. ?/11/36.
Retford 3/8/43.

RENUMBERED:
5044 26/7/24.
3230 allocated.

Tender sent to Gorton 6/12/43.

5048

Gorton.

To traffic 5/1909.

REPAIRS:
Gor. ?/?—23/8/13.**G.**
Gor. 20/3—26/6/20.**G.**

Gor. 23/9—11/11/22.**G.**
Gor. 29/3—11/10/24.**G.**
Gor. 23/10/26—15/1/27.**G.**
Gor. 2/7—6/8/27.**G.**
New L.H. cylinder.
Gor. 12/10—2/11/29.**G.**
Gor. 25/7—15/8/31.**G.**
Gor. 25/11—9/12/33.**G.**
Gor. 11/4—2/5/36.**G.**
Gor. 30/9—7/10/39.**G.**
Don. 4/1/43.
Rebuilt to Class Q1.

BOILERS:
1366.
  868 23/8/13.
1264 *(superheated)* 26/6/20.
1691 *(saturated)* 11/10/24.
1817 2/11/29.
1679 15/8/31.
  54 9/12/33.
3723 *(superheated)* 7/10/39.

SHEDS:
Mexborough 14/7/09.
Doncaster 30/4/28.
Ardsley 26/6/36.
Barnsley 10/11/37.

RENUMBERED:
5048 11/10/24.

Tender sent to Gorton 20/1/43.

5049

Gorton.

To traffic 6/1909.

REPAIRS:
Gor. ?/?—4/10/13.**G.**
Gor. ?/?—22/7/16.**G.**
Gor. 28/1—6/5/22.**G.**
Gor. 14/6—8/11/24.**G.**
Gor. 29/1—9/4/27.**G.**
Gor. 3—31/8/29.**G.**
Gor. 25/7—15/8/31.**G.**
Gor. 2—23/9/33.**G.**
Gor. 20/6—11/7/36.**G.**

BOILERS:
1367.
1412 4/10/13.
1632 *(superheated)* 22/7/16.
1817 *(saturated)* 6/5/22.
1409 8/11/24.
1841 *(saturated)* 31/8/29.
  647 15/8/31.
1777 23/9/33.
  850 11/7/36.

SHEDS:
Mexborough 13/8/09.
Sheffield 15/10/26.

Mexborough 10/12/26.
Doncaster 28/4/28.
Mexborough 23/2/34.
Langwith Jct. 16/11/36.
Mexborough 6/5/37.

RENUMBERED:
5049 8/11/24.

CONDEMNED: 17/11/39.
Into Gor. for cut up 18/11/39.

5062

Gorton.

To traffic 6/1909.

REPAIRS:
Gor. ?/?—29/11/13.**G.**
Gor. ?/?—31/5/19.**G.**
Gor. 16/7—24/9/21.**G.**
Gor. 11/8/23—16/2/24.**G.**
Gor. 21/8—6/11/26.**G.**
Gor. 25/8—22/9/28.**G.**
Gor. 23/8—4/10/30.**G.**
Gor. 28/3—11/4/31.**L.**
After collision.
Gor. 27/5—3/6/33.**G.**
Gor. 21/12/35—4/1/36.**G.**

BOILERS:
1368.
1366 29/11/13.
  929 *(superheated)* 31/5/19.
  374 *(saturated)* 16/2/24.
1267 6/11/26.
  907 *(saturated)* 22/9/28.
1772 3/6/33.
  908 4/1/36.

SHEDS:
Mexborough.
Doncaster ?/?
March *by* 13/5/28.
Immingham 2/3/29.
Keadby 10/6/29.
Sheffield 10/4/31.
Staveley 20/6/31.
Barnsley 25/1/32.

RENUMBERED:
5062 16/2/24.

CONDEMNED: 8/5/37.
Cut up at Gorton.

5063

Gorton.

To traffic 7/1909.

REPAIRS:
Gor. ?/?—25/7/14.**G.**

Gor. ?/?—10/7/20.**G.**
Gor. 17/6—19/8/22.**G.**
Gor. 17/5—26/7/24.**G.**
Gor. 16/10—25/12/26.**G.**
Gor. 9/2—23/3/29.**G.**
Gor. 27/9—18/10/30.**G.**
Gor. 27/5—10/6/33.**G.**

BOILERS:
1369.
1371 25/7/14.
  352 10/7/20.
1916 25/12/26.
  468A 23/3/29.
1138 18/10/30.
  185 *(superheated)* 10/6/33.

SHEDS:
Keadby.
Immingham 1/11/30.

RENUMBERED:
5063 26/7/24.

CONDEMNED: 22/6/36.
Into Gor. for cut up 27/6/36.

5212

Gorton.

To traffic 8/1909.

REPAIRS:
Gor. ?/?—23/1/15.**G.**
Gor. ?/?—28/2/20.**G.**
Gor. 24/12/21—18/3/22.**G.**
Gor. 28/6—23/8/24.**G.**
Gor. 31/12/26—2/7/27.**G.**
Gor. 11/1—15/2/30.**G.**
Gor. 4—18/4/31.**L.**
Gor. 4—11/2/33.**G.**
Gor. 26/10—9/11/35.**G.**

BOILERS:
1370.
1405 *(superheated)* 23/1/15.
1369 28/2/20.
  829 2/7/27.
  916 11/2/33.
  892 9/11/35.

SHEDS:
Staveley.
Barnsley 30/3/32.

RENUMBERED:
5212 23/8/24.

CONDEMNED: 12/3/38.
Cut up at Gorton.

When No.3233 was ex works 20th September 1947, it had Group Standard buffers and drawhook. Nos.63217 and 63223 were the only other Q4's so fitted.

No.63223, ex general repair on 10th April 1948, as well as having GS buffers and drawhook, also had screw adjustable coupling instead of the customary 3-link type.

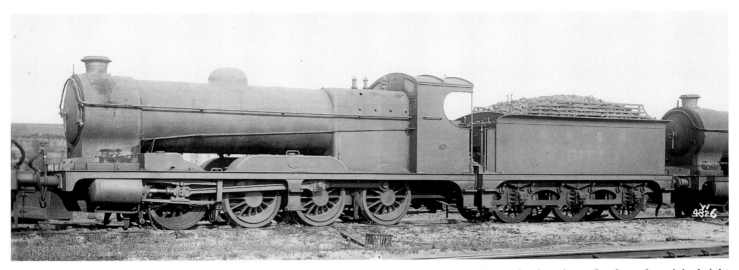

When a superheater was put in it was usual to provide mechanical lubrication to the cylinders and valves, but a few kept the original sight feed from a lubricator in the cab with inclined pipes along the left hand side of the boiler. So noted were Nos.5057, 5067, 5085, 5151 and 6135. No.5151 was recorded as changed to mechanical lubrication ex works 10th October 1936, which proved to be its final repair.

Only one Q4 had Intensifore lubrication; No.1134 being fitted in January 1916 when it got the special small-tube superheater. It then kept Intensifore until it went for repair 19th January 1935.

When ex works 9th February 1935, the Intensifore lubricator on No.6134 had been changed to a Wakefield type. Note that it had also lost the November 1927 built boiler with base cover to safety valves.

5213

Gorton.

To traffic 9/1909.

REPAIRS:
Gor. ?/?—28/2/14.**G**.
Gor. 6/11/20—8/1/21.**G**.
Gor. 20/10—29/12/23.**G**.
Gor. 13/11/26—15/1/27.**G**.
Gor. 24/8—5/10/29.**G**.
Gor. 18/4—9/5/31.**G**.
Gor. 22/7—5/8/33.**G**.
Gor. 3—17/8/35.**G**.

BOILERS:
1371.
1270 28/2/14.
1372 *(superheated)* 8/1/21.
 592 5/10/29.
 906 5/8/33.
1678 17/8/35.

SHEDS:
Sheffield.
Colwick 21/1/27.
Staveley 5/4/27.
Barnsley 29/3/32.

RENUMBERED:
5213 15/1/27 *or earlier.*

CONDEMNED: 13/7/38.
Cut up at Gorton.

5356

Gorton.

To traffic 10/1909.

REPAIRS:
Gor. ?/?—14/11/14.**G**.
Gor. ?/?—9/10/20.**G**.
Gor. 7/10—16/12/22.**G**.
Gor. 16/8—18/10/24.**G**.
Gor. 5/3—9/7/27.**G**.
Gor. 18/1—22/2/30.**G**.
Gor. 28/5—11/6/32.**G**.
Gor. 25/3—1/4/33.**G**.
Gor. 10—24/11/34.**G**.

BOILERS:
1372.
1402 *(superheated)* 14/11/14.
1918 9/10/20.
 832 11/6/32.
 839 1/4/33.
 918 24/11/34.

SHEDS:
Mexborough 11/12/09.
Ardsley 31/1/28.
Keadby 12/10/29.
Frodingham 18/6/32.

RENUMBERED:
5356 18/10/24.

CONDEMNED: 8/5/37.
Cut up at Gorton.

5159

Gorton.

To traffic 10/1909.

REPAIRS:
Gor. 27/3—23/10/15.**G**.
Superheater fitted.
Gor. 13/12/19—7/2/20.**G**.
Gor. 18/12/20—29/1/21.**G**.
Gor. 17/3—26/5/23.**G**.
Gor. 2/5—15/8/25.**G**.
Gor. 7/4—26/5/28.**G**.
Gor. 11/7—1/8/31.**G**.
Gor. 7—28/4/34.**G**.
New R.H. cylinder.
Gor. 3—17/10/36.**G**.
Gor. 29/7—12/8/39.**G**.
Gor. 8—25/10/41.**G**.
Gor. 6—16/1/43.**G**.
Gor. 21/4—19/5/45.**G**.
New cylinders.
Gor. 8/3—5/4/47.**G**.

BOILERS:
1373.
1634 7/2/20.
 54 *(saturated)* 29/1/21.
 850 *(superheated)* 26/5/28.
 837 1/8/31.
 914 28/4/34.
 185 17/10/36.
 869 12/8/39.
 838 25/10/41.
 910 16/1/43.
3737 19/5/45.
3724 5/4/47.

SHEDS:
Mexborough 11/10/12.
Sheffield 15/10/26.
Mexborough 7/12/26.
Ardsley 12/6/28.

RENUMBERED:
5159 15/8/25.
3231 23/1/46.

CONDEMNED: 20/3/50.
Into Gor. for cut up 25/3/50.

5160

Gorton.

To traffic 11/1909.

REPAIRS:
Gor. ?/?—23/10/15.**G**.
Gor. 18/12/20—22/1/21.**G**.
Gor. 17/2—2/6/23.**G**.
Gor. 16/8—1/11/24.**G**.
Gor. 16/7—22/10/27.**G**.
Gor. 16/8—27/9/30.**G**.
Gor. 21/5—25/6/32.**G**.
*New 21in. cylinders and
piston valves.*
Gor. 12—26/10/35.**G**.
Gor. 11—25/6/38.**G**.
Gor. 29/3—12/4/41.**G**.
Gor. 26/6—3/7/43.**G**.
Gor. 27/1—24/2/45.**H**.
Gor. 6—27/7/46.**L**.
Broken L.H. cylinder.
Gor. 25/10—15/11/47.**G**.
Gor. 7/8/48.**L**. *Tender only.*

BOILERS:
1374.
 869 *(superheated)* 23/10/15.
 47 *(saturated)* 22/1/21.
 836 *(superheated)* 22/10/27.
 468 25/6/32.
 874 26/10/35.
 833 25/6/38.
3725 12/4/41.
 903 3/7/43.
3736 24/2/45.
 874 15/11/47.

SHEDS:
Mexborough 11/1/13.
Keadby *after* 23/2/20.
Ardsley 1/11/27.

RENUMBERED:
5160 1/11/24.
3232 20/1/46.
63232 7/8/48.

CONDEMNED: 5/6/50.
Into Gor. for cut up 10/6/50.

5161

Gorton.

To traffic 11/1909.

REPAIRS:
Gor. ?/?—12/12/14.**G**.
Gor. 23/4—11/6/21.**G**.
Gor. 20/10/23—5/4/24.**G**.
Gor. 12/12/25—6/2/26.**G**.
Gor. 11/8—1/9/28.**G**.
Gor. 11/10—1/11/30.**G**.
Gor. 31/12/32—14/1/33.**G**.
Gor. 13—27/4/35.**G**.
Gor. 10—24/7/37.**G**.
Gor. 30/12/39—13/1/40.**G**.
Gor. 14—26/9/42.**G**.
Gor. 20/1—24/2/45.**G**.
Gor. 23/8—20/9/47.**G**.
Gor. 29/1—19/2/49.**C/H**.
*Secondhand cylinders
ex-B9 1478.*

BOILERS:
1375.
 861 *(superheated)* 12/12/14.
 439 *(saturated)* 5/4/24.
 495 *(superheated)* 1/9/28.
1911 1/11/30.
 138 14/1/33.
 907 27/4/35.
 601 24/7/37.
 832 13/1/40.
 875 26/9/42.
 852 24/2/45.
 138 20/9/47.

SHEDS:
Staveley 4/1/13.
Barnsley *by* 1935.
Langwith Jct. 27/10/46.
Barnsley 5/10/47.

RENUMBERED:
5161 5/4/24.
3233 27/1/46.
63233 19/2/49.

CONDEMNED: 6/2/50.
Into Gor. for cut up 11/2/50.

5162

Gorton.

To traffic 12/1909.

REPAIRS:
Gor. ?/?—20/3/15.**G**.
Gor. 10/7—25/12/20.**G**.
New L.H. cylinder.
Gor. 8/3—10/5/24.**G**.
Gor. 24/4—7/8/26.**G**.
Gor. 24/11/28—5/1/29.**G**.
Gor. 30/8—4/10/30.**G**.

(*above*) From 1916 No.6134 had 21in. diameter cylinders and 10in. piston valves whereas the rest had 19in. cylinders and slide valves. The LNER changed five from 1928 onwards: Nos.5136 (10/3/28), 5137 (14/1/31), 5153 (6/5/33), 5160 (25/6/32) and 6076 (4/7/31). All these had Wakefield mechanical lubrication.

(*right*) On most of the class until 1929 there was a double footstep and handgrip between the second and third pair of wheels, with a single step on the crosshead slide bar support bracket. By December 1925 however, a start had been made removing the double footstep (*see page 73, bottom*).

Just the single step proved both inadequate (too high) and unsafe, because its edges were not turned up. It was thus altered to a substantial plate with two steps.

5162 cont./
Gor. 25/3—8/4/33.**G.**
Gor. 8/12/34—12/1/35.**G.**
Gor. 24/7—7/8/37.**G.**
Secondhand R.H. cylinder.
Gor. 27/7—31/8/40.**G.**
New cylinders.
Gor. 4—20/3/43.**G.**
Gor. 13—20/5/44.**G.**
Gor. 2—16/6/45.**L.**
Gor. 16/8—6/9/47.**G.**
Gor. 9—16/4/49.**H.**

BOILERS:
1376.
844 *(superheated)* 20/3/15.
1912 25/12/20.
728 7/8/26.
1711 4/10/30.
333 8/4/33.
641 12/1/35.
913 7/8/37.
850 20/3/43.
3725 *(sup. removed)* 20/5/44.
918 *(saturated)* 6/9/47.
3774 16/4/49.

SHEDS:
Mexborough 18/10/12.
Keadby *by* 1922.
Immingham 12/10/30.
Mexborough 8/1/38.
Grantham 23/2/47.
Ardsley 4/6/50.

RENUMBERED:
5162 10/5/24.
3234 27/1/46.
63234 16/4/49.

CONDEMNED: 5/3/51.
Into Gor. for cut up 10/3/51.

5163

Gorton.

To traffic 12/1909.

REPAIRS:
Gor. ?/?—16/5/14.**G.**
Gor. ?/?—10/7/20.**G.**
Gor. 21/10—23/12/22.**G.**
Gor. 3/5—12/7/24.**G.**
Gor. 25/6—6/8/27.**G.**
Gor. 2/2—16/3/29.**G.**
Gor. 22/11—13/12/30.**G.**
Gor. 6—13/5/33.**G.**
Gor. 21/12/35—11/1/36.**G.**
New L.H. cylinder.
Gor. 25/6—9/7/38.**G.**
Gor. 25/1—8/2/41.**G.**
Gor. 8/4—1/5/43.**G.**
Gor. 11/8—8/9/45.**G.**
Secondhand R.H. cylinder.

Gor. 21/2—13/3/48.**G.**

BOILERS:
1377.
1385 16/5/14.
838 10/7/20.
1902 6/8/27.
530 16/3/29.
722 *(superheated)* 13/12/30.
651 13/5/33.
468 11/1/36.
903 9/7/38.
3727 8/2/41.
3742 1/5/43.
3741 8/9/45.
830 13/3/48.

SHEDS:
Mexborough 19/5/12.
Ardsley 17/1/28.
Keadby 10/10/29.
Immingham 12/12/30.
Lincoln 3/5/42.
New England 12/12/43.
New England MGN 27/8/44.
Langwith Jct. 28/10/45.
Barnsley 7/4/46.
Langwith Jct. 27/10/46.
Barnsley 5/10/47.

RENUMBERED:
5163 12/7/24.
3235 3/2/46.
ᴇ**3235** 13/3/48.

CONDEMNED: 7/5/51.
Into Gor. for cut up 26/5/51.

5164

Gorton.

To traffic 12/1909.

REPAIRS:
Gor. ?/?—11/4/14.**G.**
Gor. ?/?—29/11/19.**G.**
Gor. 3/12/21—11/2/22.**G.**
Gor. 1/3—28/6/24.**G.**
Gor. 23/10/26—15/1/27.**G.**
Gor. 25/8—29/9/28.**G.**
Gor. 16/5—6/6/31.**G.**
Gor. 3—17/2/34.**G.**
Gor. 30/5—20/6/36.**G.**
Gor. 15—29/10/38.**G.**
Gor. 27/4—25/5/40.**G.**
After collision.
Gor. 24/2—13/3/43.**G.**
Gor. 3—8/1/44.**L.**
New R.H. cylinder.
Gor. 24/11—8/12/45.**G.**
Gor. 24/4—15/5/48.**G.**
New L.H. cylinder.

BOILERS:
1378.
352 11/4/14.
1822 29/11/19.
550 28/6/24.
910 *(superheated)* 29/9/28.
552 6/6/31.
834 17/2/34.
47 20/6/36.
893 29/10/38.
838 13/3/43.
3742 8/12/45.
3734 15/5/48.

SHEDS:
Mexborough 27/4/12.
Keadby *after* 1923.
Frodingham 18/6/32.
Barnsley 19/2/39.
Ardsley 4/5/39.

RENUMBERED:
5164 28/6/24.
3236 24/2/46.
63236 15/5/48.

CONDEMNED: 26/5/51.
Cut up at Gorton.

5401

Gorton.

To traffic 6/1910.

REPAIRS:
Gor. 1/7—16/12/16.**G.**
Shipped to France 17/4/17.
Returned to UK 16/5/19.
Gor. 28/6—9/8/19.**G.**
Gor. 23/7—22/10/21.**G.**
Gor. 4/8/23—2/2/24.**G.**
Gor. 27/3—5/6/26.**G.**
Gor. 10/11/28—26/1/29.**G.**
Gor. 7—21/3/31.**G.**
Gor. 16—30/6/34.**G.**

BOILERS:
1399.
866 22/10/21.
336 2/2/24.
312 26/1/29.
1832 21/3/31.
201 30/6/34.

SHED:
Mexborough.

RENUMBERED:
5401 2/2/24.

CONDEMNED: 22/12/37.
Cut up at Gorton.

5956

Gorton.

To traffic 8/1910.

REPAIRS:
Gor. ?/?—29/5/15.**G.**
Gor. ?/?—31/7/20.**G.**
Gor. 11/11/22—13/1/23.**G.**
Gor. 31/1—18/4/25.**G.**
Gor. 28/1—31/3/28.**G.**
Gor. 2/11—7/12/29.**G.**
Gor. 10—31/10/31.**G.**
Gor. 30/6—14/7/34.**G.**
Gor. 6—20/3/37.**G.**
Gor. 7—21/8/37.**H.**

BOILERS:
1404.
1271 *(superheated)* 29/5/15.
1903 31/7/20.
1920 31/3/28.
1916 31/10/31.
842 14/7/34.
1920 20/3/37.
907 21/8/37.

SHEDS:
Keadby.
Immingham 7/11/31.

RENUMBERED:
5956 18/4/25.

CONDEMNED: 4/7/39.

5957

Gorton.

To traffic 8/1910.

REPAIRS:
Gor. ?/?—24/10/14.**G.**
Gor. ?/?—1/11/19.**G.**
Gor. 21/1—11/3/22.**G.**
Gor. 14/7—15/12/23.**G.**
Gor. 28/2—2/5/25.**G.**
Gor. 27/8—26/11/27.**G.**
Gor. 12/10—16/11/29.**G.**
Gor. 26/9—17/10/31.**G.**
Gor. 10—24/3/34.**G.**
Gor. 18/4/36. *Not repaired.*

BOILERS:
1405.
1365 24/10/14.
1817 1/11/19.
1272 11/3/22.
319 15/12/23.
47 *(superheated)* 26/11/27.
911 17/10/31.
640 24/3/34.

The first 41 engines had 3250 gallons tenders with four open coal rails and on 22nd March 1924 No.6141 changed to one of them (T5145) which it then had to 5th April 1930, before reverting to 4000 gallons type. Nos.1133 to 1144 had this capacity from new but originally also with four open coal rails.

Beginning in February 1909 with No.39, the final 35 engines had 4000 gallons tender but with solid coal guard which had half-round beading to the edge. Note No.5044 still had its number on the tender until it went to works on 15th December 1934 although it had a general repair in May 1931.

5957 cont./
SHED:
Langwith Jct.

RENUMBERED:
5957 2/5/25.

CONDEMNED: 28/4/36.
Cut up at Gorton.

5958

Gorton.

To traffic 8/1910.

REPAIRS:
Gor. ?/?—24/6/16.**G.**
Gor. 6/11—25/12/20.**G.**
Gor. 17/2—7/4/23.**G.**
Gor. 2/8—18/10/24.**G.**
Gor. 27/8—10/12/27.**G.**
Gor. 29/3—26/4/30.**G.**
Gor. 12—19/11/32.**G.**
Gor. 19/1—2/2/35.**G.**

BOILERS:
1406.
237 (superheated) 24/6/16.
40 (saturated) 25/12/20.
1400 (superheated) 10/12/27.
903 26/4/30.
1682 19/11/32.
1918 2/2/35.

SHEDS:
Mexborough.
Doncaster ?/24.
Mexborough 19/5/25.
Langwith Jct. 7/5/30.

RENUMBERED:
5958 18/10/24.

CONDEMNED: 5/3/37.
Into Gor. for cut up 6/3/37.

5959

Gorton.

To traffic 9/1910.

REPAIRS:
Gor. ?/?—27/2/15.**G.**
Gor. ?/?—14/8/20.**G.**
Gor. 17/6—16/9/22.**G.**
Gor. 2/2—22/3/24.**G.**
Gor. 26/6—6/11/26.**G.**
Gor. 19/1—23/2/29.**G.**
Gor. 14—28/2/31.**G.**
Gor. 30/12/33—13/1/34.**G.**
Gor. 4—18/7/36.**G.**
Gor. 20/5—3/6/39.**G.**

Gor. 16/10—1/11/41.**G.**
Gor. 24/7—1/8/42.**L.**
Suspected loose wheel.
Don. 17/1/44.
Rebuilt to Class Q1.

BOILERS:
1407.
1375 (superheated) 27/2/15.
1405 14/8/20.
1912 6/11/26.
640 28/2/31.
851 13/1/34.
831 18/7/36.
643 3/6/39.
3731 1/11/41.

SHEDS:
Langwith Jct. 21/6/13.
Ardsley 18/5/31.

RENUMBERED:
5959 22/3/24.
3237 allocated.

Tender sent to Gorton 14/4/44.

5960

Gorton.

To traffic 10/1910.

REPAIRS:
Gor. ?/12/15—15/7/16.**G.**
Superheater installed.
Gor. 17/7—16/10/20.**G.**
Gor. 9/12/22—3/2/23.**G.**
Gor. 6/12/24—28/2/25.**G.**
Gor. 12/11—24/12/27.**G.**
Gor. 18/1—22/2/30.**G.**
Gor. 5—19/3/32.**G.**

BOILERS:
1408.
1920 16/10/20.
891 24/12/27.
336 19/3/32.

SHEDS:
Mexborough.
Doncaster ?/24.
Mexborough 17/2/34.

RENUMBERED:
5960 28/2/25.

CONDEMNED: 2/5/36.
Cut up at Gorton.

5961

Gorton.

To traffic 11/1910.

REPAIRS:
Gor. 11/6—13/8/21.**G.**
Gor. 9/6—7/7/23.**G.**
Gor. 29/8—24/10/25.**G.**
Gor. 28/1—10/3/28.**G.**
Gor. 12/4—3/5/30.**G.**
Gor. 9—16/7/32.**G.**
Gor. 18/8—1/9/34.**G.**
Gor. 31/12/36—16/1/37.**G.**
Gor. 24/6—8/7/39.**G.**
Don. 6/10/42.
Rebuilt to Class Q1.

BOILERS:
1411.
1266 13/8/21.
1711 24/10/25.
1822 3/5/30.
431 16/7/32.
1832 1/9/34.
905 (superheated) 16/1/37.
912 8/7/39.

SHEDS:
Mexborough 15/9/16.
Doncaster 16/2/24.
Frodingham 31/1/36.
Mexborough 22/8/39.

RENUMBERED:
5961 24/10/25.

Tender sent to Gorton 1/1/43.

5962

Gorton.

To traffic 11/1910.

REPAIRS:
Gor. ?/?—9/8/13.**G.**
Gor. 15/6—9/11/18.**G.**
New R.H. cylinder.
Gor. 21/5—25/6/21.**G.**
Gor. 28/7/23—5/1/24.**G.**
Gor. 19/11/27—14/1/28.**G.**
Gor. 19/7—16/8/30.**G.**
Gor. 13—27/5/33.**G.**
Gor. 28/12/35—18/1/36.**G.**
Gor. 29/1—12/2/38.**G.**
Gor. 30/11—14/12/40.**G.**
New L.H. cylinder.
Gor. 9—18/9/43.**H.**
Gor. 22/3—26/4/47.**G.**

BOILERS:
1412.
853 9/8/13.

842 9/11/18.
333 5/1/24.
40 14/1/28.
54 16/8/30.
312 27/5/33.
3721 (superheated) 18/1/36.
728 12/2/38.
891 14/12/40.
468 18/9/43.
3730 26/4/47.

SHEDS:
Mexborough 8/2/11.
Doncaster 31/1/24.
March 14/7/25.
Staveley 14/3/29.
Barnsley 5/9/43.
Langwith Jct. 23/9/44.
Barnsley 7/4/46.
Langwith Jct. 27/10/46.
Barnsley 5/10/47.

RENUMBERED:
5962 2/24?
3238 10/11/46.

CONDEMNED: 6/2/50.
Into Gor. for cut up 11/2/50.

5963

Gorton.

To traffic 12/1910.

REPAIRS:
Gor. 26/4—5/7/13.**G.**
Gor. 21/8/15—26/2/16.**G.**
Gor. 18/9—27/11/20.**G.**
Gor. 24/2—19/5/23.**G.**
Gor. 28/11/25—30/1/26.**G.**
Gor. 15/12/28—26/1/29.**G.**
Gor. 28/2—21/3/31.**G.**
Gor. 10—31/3/34.**G.**

BOILERS:
1413.
1414 (superheated) 26/2/16.
862 (saturated) 27/11/20.
651 (superheated) 30/1/26.
914 21/3/31.
552 31/3/34.

SHEDS:
Mexborough.
Doncaster ?/24.
March 24/1/29.
Annesley 9/3/29.
Ardsley 22/5/31.

RENUMBERED:
5963 30/1/26.

CONDEMNED: 3/10/36.
Cut up at Gorton.

All had tender fitted with water pick-up gear as shown by the spoked handwheel for operating it at the right hand front edge of the tender.

Late in 1939, instructions were issued for pick-up gear to be removed from Q4 tenders and No.5059, ex works 21st October 1939 (*see* page 47, middle) was probably the first to lose it. Between 13th January and 15th June 1940 ten, Nos.5056, 5065, 5070, 5085, 5138, 5142, 5161, 5164, 6133 and 6139, had w.p.u. gear removed before the instruction was cancelled. It was re-issued in March 1946 and the thirty-four survivors would lose it as all had a least one later works visit.

The tenders with open coal rails gradually had them plated. When this was done by the GCR the plate was put on the outside of the rails and had no beading to the edge. The LNER made an effort to change the first forty-one Q4's from 3250 to 4000 gallons type and when No.5058 changed in January 1929 only No.6074 still had a 3250 gallons type and it got the higher capacity tender from October 1930.

When the plating was done after Grouping, it was fitted on the inside of the rails, which could then still be seen. Ex works 12th April 1924, No.6053 had the original tender from D9 class 5105 which changed it from 3250 to 4000 gallons, and had it plated inside the rails.

Although originally with double lining (*see* page 50, middle) at Grouping they were all plain black and did not carry the GC company's crest.

From February 1923 they were entitled to have red lining, but few (if any) had this applied. Painting of this class had a very low rating as shown by photos of Nos.5401 and 5044 (*see* pages 36 and 40, bottom) which in February and July 1924 were only touched up.

The Painting Economies of June 1928 thus did not affect Q4 class and No.5091, newly superheated and ex works 13th October 1928, just had the usual one coat of black paint. Nor was there any hurry to move the number to the cab when this began to take place from March 1929. No.5044 to December 1934 (*see* page 69, bottom) still had tender number, and No.5960 (*see* page 59, bottom) which was withdrawn 2nd May 1936 never got cab numbering. Note single step still in place but central steps removed.

5964

Gorton.

To traffic 12/1910.

REPAIRS:
Gor. 7/8/15—19/2/16.**G.**
Gor. 1/10—26/11/21.**G.**
Gor. 8/3—28/6/24.**G.**
Gor. 30/7—17/9/27.**G.**
Gor. 6/4—4/5/29.**G.**
Gor. 18/7—8/8/31.**G.**
Gor. 11/11—2/12/33.**G.**
Gor. 14—28/3/36.**G.**

BOILERS:
1414.
1413 (superheated) 19/2/16.
1399 (saturated) 26/11/21.
1822 28/6/24.
1916 4/5/29.
1650 (superheated) 8/8/31.
840 2/12/33.
1696 28/3/36.

SHEDS:
Immingham.
Ardsley 1/10/27.
Keadby 10/10/29.
Frodingham 18/6/32.

RENUMBERED:
5964 28/6/24.

CONDEMNED: 30/8/38.
Cut up at Gorton.

5965

Gorton.

To traffic 12/1910.

REPAIRS:
Gor. 11/12/15—24/6/16.**G.**
Superheater installed.
Gor. 19/3—25/6/21.**G.**
Gor. 28/7—20/10/23.**G.**
Gor. 27/2—5/6/26.**G.**
Gor. 10/12/27—18/2/28.**G.**
Gor. 17/5—21/6/30.**G.**
Gor. 13—27/8/32.**G.**
Gor. 13/1—3/2/34.**G.**
Gor. 19/9—3/10/36.**G.**

BOILERS:
1415.
237 25/6/21.
898 18/2/28.
834 27/8/32.
910 3/2/34.
3725 3/10/36.

SHEDS:
Mexborough.
Doncaster ?/24.
Ardsley 13/11/34.

RENUMBERED:
5965 5/6/26 or earlier.

CONDEMNED: 29/10/38.
Cut up at Gorton.

6174

Gorton.

To traffic 6/1910.

REPAIRS:
Gor. 26/6—13/11/15.**G.**
Superheater installed.
Gor. 31/7—11/12/20.**G.**
Gor. 25/11/22—20/1/23.**G.**
Gor. 17/1—21/3/25.**G.**
Gor. 11/2—31/3/28.**G.**
Gor. 25/10—22/11/30.**G.**
Gor. 19/8—2/9/33.**G.**

BOILERS:
1400.
1271 11/12/20.
165 31/3/28.
495 22/11/30.
592 2/9/33.

SHEDS:
Mexborough.
Ardsley 16/4/28.
Bradford 2/3/31.
Ardsley 4/6/31.

RENUMBERED:
6174 21/3/25.

CONDEMNED: 5/6/36.
Into Gor. for cut up 6/6/36.

6175

Gorton.

To traffic 6/1910.

REPAIRS:
Gor. 5/6/15—29/1/16.**G.**
Superheater installed.
Mex. 18/2—12/10/20.**H.**
Gor. 5/8/22—13/1/23.**G.**
Gor. 19/1—15/3/24.**G.**
Gor. 9/10/26—12/3/27.**G.**
Gor. 11/5—8/6/29.**G.**
Gor. 3—24/10/31.**G.**
Gor. 2—16/2/35.**G.**
Gor. 2—23/4/38.**G.**
Gor. 18/1—1/2/41.**G.**
Gor. 5/6/43. Not repaired.

BOILERS:
1401.
858 13/1/23.
1701 12/3/27.
1841 24/10/31.
1682 16/2/35.
898 24/3/38.
3726 1/2/41.

SHEDS:
Mexborough 21/8/10.
Ardsley 19/11/36.

RENUMBERED:
6175 15/3/24.
3239 allocated.

CONDEMNED: 19/7/43.
Cut up at Gorton.

6176

Gorton.

To traffic 7/1910.

REPAIRS:
Gor. ?/?—8/8/14.**G.**
Gor. ?/?—6/7/18.**G.**
Gor. 10/6—2/12/22.**G.**
Gor. 5/4—31/5/24.**G.**
Gor. 6/2—22/5/26.**G.**
Gor. 12/5—30/6/28.**G.**
Gor. 15/3—5/4/30.**G.**
Gor. 30/4—14/5/32.**G.**
Gor. 24/11—8/12/34.**G.**
Gor. 30/3—4/5/35.**L.**
New R.H. cylinder.
Gor. 13—27/3/37.**G.**
Gor. 15—29/7/39.**G.**
New L.H. cylinder.
Gor. 14/11—20/12/41.**G.**
Gor. 6—16/5/44.**G.**
Gor. 25/1—22/2/47.**G.**
Gor. 19—26/2/49.**H.**
Tablet exchange apparatus
fitted.

BOILERS:
1402.
1378 8/8/14.
1267 6/7/18.
1610 (superheated) 2/12/22.
903 30/6/28.
896 5/4/30.
847 14/5/32.
896 8/12/34.
842 27/3/37.
145 29/7/39.
848 20/12/41.
3730 16/5/44.
908 22/2/47.
3726 26/2/49.

SHEDS:
Langwith Jct..
Retford 3/8/43.
New England 12/12/43.
New England MGN 27/8/44.
Retford 28/10/45.
Grantham 13/10/46.
Ardsley 4/6/50.

RENUMBERED:
6176 31/5/24.
3240 3/11/46.
63240 26/2/49.

CONDEMNED: 13/6/51.
Into Gor. for cut up 16/6/51.

6177

Gorton.

To traffic 7/1910.

REPAIRS:
Gor. ?/?—30/11/18.**G.**
Gor. 18/6—17/9/21.**G.**
Gor. 29/9/23—8/3/24.**G.**
Gor. 15/10—10/12/27.**G.**
Gor. 16—23/3/29.**L.**
Gor. 9—30/11/29.**G.**
Gor. 13—27/6/31.**G.**
Gor. 11—25/11/33.**G.**
Gor. 25/7—8/8/36.**G.**
Gor. 8—15/7/39.**G.**
Gor. 7—24/1/42.**G.**
Gor. 6—31/7/43.**H.**
New R.H. cylinder.
Gor. 26/5—16/6/45.**G.**
Gor. 7—28/6/47.**G.**

BOILERS:
1403.
857 30/11/18.
419 8/3/24.
129 30/11/29.
201 27/6/31.
439 25/11/33.
129 8/8/36.
19 15/7/39.
374 24/1/42.
913 31/7/43.
918 16/6/45.
3769 28/6/47.

SHEDS:
Mexborough 4/10/10.
Doncaster 18/3/24.
March 15/7/25.
Immingham 3/3/29.
Keadby 20/9/29.
Doncaster 3/12/29.
Bradford 21/11/34.
Ardsley 2/2/41.

Until July 1942 this was then standard style livery with figures and letters all put on by 12in. shaded transfers.

War shortage of labour caused LNER on the tender to be cut to NE only until after January 1946. No.5162 was ex works 20th May 1944 with NE which it kept to 16th August 1947 having been renumbered 3234 on Sunday 27th January 1946 at Mexborough shed. As with other changes, Q4 lagged behind and from a general repair 23rd January 1943, No.5059 was ex works still with LNER (*see* page 47, middle) as shown in picture taken on 5th August 1945.

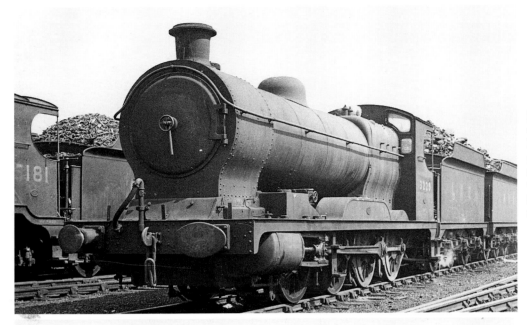

No.5039 was rather similar. Ex works 4th September 1943 its LNER lettering on the tender was undisturbed, and it did not go to works again until 7th June 1947 when LNER was again the rule. Meanwhile on Sunday 14th July 1946 Mexborough renumbered the engine to 3229.

The small stencil renumbering carried out at sheds were replaced by normal shaded transfers when the engine next went for repair. When the LNER became defunct at the end of 1947 only eight of the thirty-four survivors, Nos.3204, 3217, 3221, 3223, 3226, 3235, 3236 and 3243, had not had LNER restored. They had last had major repair between 21st April and 22nd December 1945. No.3240 was ex works on 22nd February 1947 as shown here.

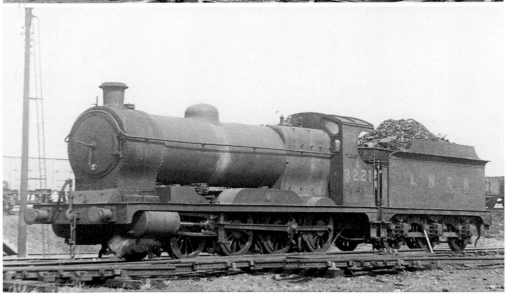

One more was to get LNER and number in shaded transfers. No.3221 was out from a general repair on 24th January 1948 but with BR Regional prefix E above the cab number. Two other Q4 got the E prefix: E3235 and E3243 both out on 13th March 1948 but with BRITISH RAILWAYS on the tender, and prefix in front of the number.

Between 10th April 1948 (63223 - *see* page 63, bottom) and 16th April 1949 (63234 - *see* page 47, top) no less than sixteen others got full BR number with BRITISH RAILWAYS on the tender. Nos.63216, 63217, 63223, 63232 and 63236 never acquired a smokebox number plate, the first to do so, out 9th October 1948, was No.63200 (*see* page 48, middle) in addition No.ᴇ3243 became 63243 out from a general repair 23rd April 1949, the last to have one.

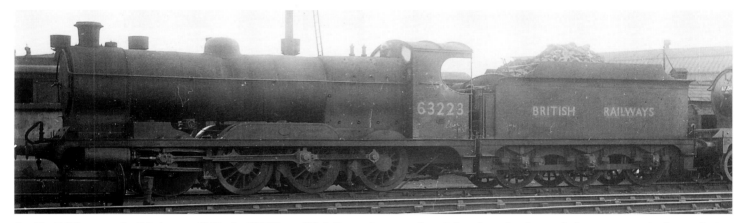

On No.63232, ex works 7th August 1948, the LNER modified figure 6 was used, and the plates for the smokebox were cast in that style (*see* page 47, top). Curiously, none of these plates, or BR cab numbers, included the figure 9.

Starting with No.63200, ex works 9th October 1948 (*see* page 48, middle) cab numbers and tender letters matched at 10in. and true Gill sans 6 was used on the cab figures.

6177 cont./
RENUMBERED:
6177 8/3/24.
3241 20/10/46.

CONDEMNED: 17/4/50.
Into Gor. for cut up 22/4/50.

6178

Gorton.

To traffic 10/1910.

REPAIRS:
Gor. 19/2—19/8/16.**G.**
Gor. 18/10—6/12/19.**G.**
Gor. 3/12/21—11/2/22.**G.**
Gor. 8/12/23—16/2/24.**G.**
Gor. 10/10—12/12/25.**G.**
Gor. 14/7—18/8/28.**G.**
Gor. 7—28/12/29.**G.**
Gor. 26/11—3/12/32.**G.**
Gor. 7—14/3/36.**G.**
Gor. 26/9—10/10/36.**L.**

BOILERS:
1409.
1634 *(superheated)* 19/8/16.
1272 *(saturated)* 6/12/19.
844 *(superheated)* 11/2/22.
650 12/12/25.
370 28/12/29.
897 3/12/32.
832 14/3/36.

SHEDS:
Mexborough 29/4/11.
Keadby *by* 1922.
Ardsley 31/12/29.
Bradford 4/10/30.

RENUMBERED:
6178 16/2/24.

CONDEMNED: 15/8/39.
Cut up at Gorton.

6179

Gorton.

To traffic 11/1910.

REPAIRS:
Gor. 6/2—12/6/15.**G.**
Gor. 31/1—17/4/20.**G.**
Gor. 2/9/22—24/2/23.**G.**
Gor. 15/11/24—3/1/25.**G.**
Gor. 27/8—3/12/27.**G.**
Gor. 11/1—8/2/30.**G.**
Gor. 17/6—1/7/33.**G.**
Gor. 30/11—14/12/35.**G.**
Gor. 27/11—11/12/37.**G.**

Gor. 13/7—3/8/40.**G.**
Gor. 5—19/10/40.**L.**
After derailment.
Gor. 6—24/10/42.**G.**
Don. 3/3/45.
Rebuilt to Class Q1.

BOILERS:
1410.
838 *(superheated)* 12/6/15.
195 *(saturated)* 17/4/20.
1400 *(superheated)* 24/2/23.
840 3/12/27.
1677 1/7/33.
893 14/12/35.
1841 11/12/36.
849 3/8/40.
725 24/10/42.

SHEDS:
Langwith Jct..
Annesley 10/3/24.
Langwith Jct. 15/4/36.
Retford 3/8/43.
New England 12/12/43.
New England MGN 27/8/44.

RENUMBERED:
6179 3/1/25.
3242 allocated.

6180

Gorton.

To traffic 1/1911.

REPAIRS:
Gor. 26/8/16—3/3/17.**G.**
Shipped to France 24/4/17.
Returned UK 13/6/19.
Gor. 19/7—23/8/19.**G.**
Gor. 30/7—29/10/21.**G.**
Gor. 22/9/23—23/2/24.**G.**
Gor. 22/10—3/12/27.**G.**
Gor. 21/12/29—18/1/30.**G.**
Gor. 5—26/7/30.**L.**
New L.H. cylinder.
Gor. 19/3—2/4/32.**G.**
Gor. 23/6—7/7/34.**G.**
Gor. 6—20/6/36.**G.**
Gor. 5—12/8/39.**G.**
Gor. 8—24/10/42.**G.**
Gor. 24/2—10/3/45.**G.**
Gor. 21/2—13/3/48.**G.**
Gor. 9—23/4/49.**G.**

BOILERS:
1416.
1409 3/3/17.
1691 29/10/21.
407 23/2/24.
431 18/1/30.
442 2/4/32.

522 7/7/34.
438 20/6/36.
918 *(superheated)* 12/8/39.
3735 24/10/42.
903 10/3/45.
3737 13/3/48.
3777 23/4/49.

SHEDS:
Mexborough 15/11/19.
Doncaster 18/3/24.
March 15/7/25.
Langwith Jct. 2/3/29.
Mexborough 7/5/37.
Grantham 23/2/47.
Ardsley 11/6/50.

RENUMBERED:
6180 23/2/24.
3243 1/9/46.
E**3243** 13/3/48.
63243 23/4/49.

CONDEMNED: 15/10/51.
Cut up at Gorton.

6181

Gorton.

To traffic 1/1911.

REPAIRS:
Gor. 4/12/15—10/6/16.**G.**
Gor. 1/10—19/11/21.**G.**
Gor. 15/12/23—31/5/24.**G.**
Gor. 24/7—9/10/26.**G.**
Gor. 22/12/28—16/2/29.**G.**
Gor. 14—28/2/31.**G.**
Gor. 11—18/3/33.**G.**
Gor. 28/3—11/4/36.**G.**

BOILERS:
1417.
1412 *(superheated)* 10/6/16.
1409 *(saturated)* 19/11/21.
525 31/5/24.
914 *(superheated)* 16/2/29.
333 28/2/31.
1632 18/3/33.
840 11/4/36.

SHEDS:
Immingham.
Doncaster 6/4/27.
Mexborough 17/2/34.
Langwith Jct. 4/12/36.
Ardsley 9/3/37.

RENUMBERED:
6181 31/5/24.

CONDEMNED: 16/3/39.
Cut up at Gorton.

6182

Gorton.

To traffic 2/1911.

REPAIRS:
Gor. 26/2—14/10/16.**G.**
Shipped to France 24/4/17.
Returned to UK 8/6/19.
Gor. 12/7—9/8/19.**G.**
Gor. 12/3—30/4/21.**G.**
Gor. 14/7—22/12/23.**G.**
Gor. 29/8—31/10/25.**G.**
Gor. 5/5—9/6/28.**G.**
Gor. 17/1—7/2/31.**G.**
Gor. 11—25/11/33.**G.**
Gor. 20/6—4/7/36.**G.**

BOILERS:
1418.
328 22/12/23.
851 *(superheated)* 9/6/28.
589 7/2/31.
831 25/11/33.
834 4/7/36.

SHEDS:
Mexborough.
Ardsley 30/6/28.

RENUMBERED:
6182 31/10/25.

CONDEMNED: 16/5/39.
Cut up at Gorton.

E3243 from 13th March 1948 here, outside the Erecting shop at Gorton, has just taken that number having been 3243 from 1st September 1946 and 6180 from 23rd February 1924. Mexborough sent it to Doncaster 8th March 1924 who passed it to March on 15th July 1925. Langwith got it 2nd March 1929 until 7th May 1937 when Mexborough had it again. On 23rd February 1947 it moved to Grantham and ex works 23rd April 1949 it became 63243. Taken out of stock 15th October 1951, its withdrawal made Class Q4 extinct. None ever had the BR emblem.

Three more, Nos.5961 (21/11/42), 6139 (26/12/42) and 5048 (20/3/43) were converted similarly. On these first four the coal capacity was 4½ tons and the tanks held 1500 gallons. From December 1946 they were given Part 1 of the class.

From November 1943 to September 1945 nine others were converted: 5070 (13/11/43), 6077 (11/12/43), 5044 (28/1/44), 5959 (4/3/44), 5087 (20/5/44), 5068 (6/9/44), 5147 (16/1/45), 6179 (28/4/45) and 5138 (8/9/45). These had 6in. longer frames, with a longer bunker to take a supplementary water tank. Coal capacity was reduced to 4 tons but the water capacity became 2000 gallons. From December 1946 these nine were Part 2 of the class.

On the first three the vertical handrails at the cab entrance were fitted externally giving a clear entrance width of 2ft 0in.

CLASS Q 1 Tank

5058

Doncaster, rebuilt from Q4.

To traffic 25/6/1942.

REPAIRS:
Cow. 26/3—18/4/45.**G.**
Cow. 5—9/2/46.**L.**
Cow. 27—28/2/46.**L.**
Cow. 24/12/47—10/1/48.**G.**
Cow. 30/1—3/3/51.**H/I.**
Cow. 12—17/3/51.**N/C.**

BOILER:
916.
916 reno.22997 3/3/51.

SHEDS:
Doncaster 2/7/42.
Frodingham 11/7/42.
Langwith Jct. 9/11/42.
Eastfield 26/8/43.

RENUMBERED:
 9925 24/11/46.
69925 3/3/51.

CONDEMNED: 13/8/54.
Cut up at Cowlairs.

5961

Doncaster, rebuilt from Q4.

To traffic 21/11/1942.

REPAIRS:
Don. 20—26/9/43.**L.**
Gor. 1/12/45—5/1/46.**G.**
Gor. 7/8—11/9/48.**G.**
Gor. 15/12/51—25/1/52.**G.**
Gor. 21/8—1/10/54.**G.**
Gor. 17/3—19/5/55.**N/C.**
Gor. 20/1/58. *Not repaired.*

BOILERS:
 3739.
 3762 11/9/48.
 22988 25/1/52.
 22985 1/10/54.

SHEDS:
March 23/11/42.
Cambridge 1/10/45.
March 21/10/48.
Frodingham 8/4/51.

RENUMBERED:
 9926 11/8/46.
69926 11/9/48.

CONDEMNED: 3/2/58.
Cut up at Gorton.

6139

Doncaster, rebuilt from Q4.

To traffic 26/12/1942.

REPAIRS:
Cow. 9—10/4/45.**L.**
Cow. 26/10/45.**N/C.**
Cow. 19/2—23/3/46.**H.**
Cow. 18/6—15/7/48.**G.**
Cow. 22—26/7/48.**N/C.**
Cow. 14—18/9/48.**L.**
Cow. 4/12/51—26/1/52.**G.**
Cow. 22—25/9/52.**N/C.**
Efd. 18—31/8/54.**C/L.**
Cow. 13—21/10/54.**C/L.**
Cow. 8—26/12/54.**C/L.**

BOILERS:
3740.
3740 reno.22998 26/1/52.

SHEDS:
Langwith Jct..
Eastfield 31/3/43.
Langwith Jct. 21/4/43.
Eastfield 26/8/43.

RENUMBERED:
 9927 23/3/46.
69927 15/7/48.

CONDEMNED: 18/4/56.
Cut up at Cowlairs 27/7/56.

5048

Doncaster, rebuilt from Q4.

To traffic 20/3/1943.

REPAIRS:
Gor. 24/2—10/3/45.**L.**
Gor. 1/9—6/10/45.**G.**
Gor. 17/1—7/2/48.**H.**
Gor. 23/7—20/8/49.**G.**
Gor. 20/11—16/12/50.**C/H.**
Gor. 21/12/52—31/1/53.**G.**
Gor. 5—18/2/53.**N/C.**
Gor. 21/8—12/10/57.**G.**

Gor. 15—19/10/57.**N/C.**

BOILERS:
 912.
3762 6/10/45.
3744 7/2/48.
3763 20/8/49.
22981 16/12/50.
22991 31/1/53.
22984 12/10/57.

SHEDS:
Barnsley.
Langwith Jct. 13/4/43.
Immingham 28/8/44.
Langwith Jct. 1/10/44.
Frodingham 15/6/58.

RENUMBERED:
 9928 7/4/46.
69928 20/8/49.

CONDEMNED: 20/8/59.
Into Dar. for cut up 22/8/59.

5070

Doncaster, rebuilt from Q4.

To traffic 13/11/1943.

REPAIRS:
Gor. 30/3—4/5/46.**G.**
Gor. 4/9—2/10/48.**G.**
Gor. 26/6—25/8/51.**G.**
Gor. 11/8—15/10/55.**G.**

BOILERS:
3744.
3763 4/5/46.
3739 2/10/48.
22986 25/8/51.
22989 15/10/55.

SHEDS:
Retford.
Langwith Jct. 19/12/43.
Immingham 9/5/44.
Langwith Jct. 15/10/44.
Frodingham 15/6/58.

RENUMBERED:
 9929 4/5/46.
69929 2/10/48.

CONDEMNED: 28/8/59.
Into Dar. for cut up 29/8/59.

6077

Doncaster, rebuilt from Q4.

To traffic 11/12/1943.

REPAIRS:
Gor. 25/1—15/2/47.**G.**
Gor. 8/10—19/11/49.**G.**
New cylinders.
Gor. 10/8—6/9/52.**G.**
Gor. 9—17/9/52.**N/C.**
Gor. 1/4—14/5/55.**H/I.**
Gor. 17—18/5/55.**N/C.**

BOILERS:
3743.
3764 15/2/47.
3744 19/11/49.
22990 6/9/52.

SHEDS:
Mexborough.
Langwith Jct. 13/2/44.
Immingham 9/5/44.
Mexborough 13/9/44.
Doncaster 25/8/46.
Frodingham 24/9/46.
Stratford 16/4/50.
Frodingham 27/8/50.

RENUMBERED:
 9930 26/5/46.
69930 19/11/49.

CONDEMNED: 2/10/58.
Into Gor. for cut up 4/10/58.

5044

Doncaster, rebuilt from Q4.

To traffic 28/1/1944.

REPAIRS:
Don. 4—10/11/44.**L.**
Tanks leaking.
Dar. 12—28/9/46.**L.**
Tank side fractured.
Dar. 5/8—19/9/47.**G.**
Dar. 4/9—7/10/50.**G.**
Gor. 17/2—9/4/55.**G.**
Gor. 20/11/58. *Not repaired.*

BOILERS:
3723.
22994 7/10/50.

WORKS CODES:- Cw - Cowlairs. Dar- Darlington. Don - Doncaster. Ghd - Gateshead. Gor - Gorton. Inv - Inverurie. Str - Stratford.
REPAIR CODES:- **C/H** - Casual Heavy. **C/L** - Casual Light. **G** - General. **H**- Heavy. **H/I** - Heavy Intermediate. **L** - Light. **L/I** - Light Intermediate. **N/C** - Non-Classified.

81

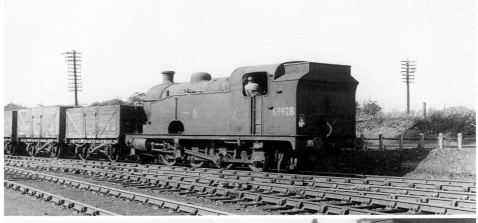

The fourth conversion No.5048 (later 9928), which was the last Part 1, and all the Part 2 engines, had the vertical handrails mounted in the cab entrance which cut the width to 1ft 1½in.

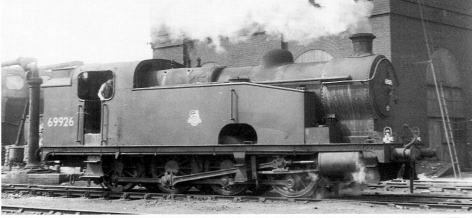

The first three engines kept the external handrails and the wider entrance, not being brought into line with the other ten.

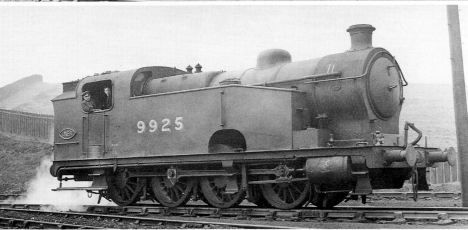

The boiler on No.5058 (later 9925) had been built in November 1929 to Diagram 17 and had started work on B5 class No.5186 in June 1931. It was put on No.5058 in March 1939. During the conversion Doncaster took out the superheater and shortened the barrel to suit the tank engine making it Diagram 17A. Nos.5044, 5048 and 5087 also got older shortened boilers when they were converted.

To suit the order given to Doncaster in April 1942 to convert another twenty-four like No.5058, Gorton provided twenty-six new Diagram 17A boilers, the extra two to permit exchange. Most had a dome cover of the usual shape but Nos.9934 and 9936 got the angular type which Gorton introduced during wartime conditions.

Standard safety valves were the tall Ross 'pop' type, and the short 'pops' put on No.9925, ex Cowlairs 10th January 1948 (*see* opposite) had gone by this 12th June 1950 photograph. They were reported as changed by October 1948.

The other Scottish based Q1 was also singular in having a rectangular casing at the base of its safety valves. This was put on when ex works 26th January 1952.

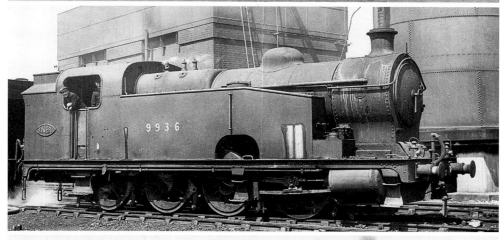

When converted, the original GC type smokebox was retained. This had wheel and handle for door fastening and the upper lamp iron was fixed on the front plate, above the door.

By February 1947 (*see* page 84, centre) the wheel was being replaced by a second handle and by August 1948 the lamp iron was being moved on to the door for easier access.

Except for one, the engines chosen for conversion had all been fitted with a superheater so the chimney was in a forward position on the smokebox. The chimney was a new one of the type used on Classes J2 and N1.

Class Q4 No.6077 had been superheated until October 1940, but ex works 30th November 1940, the superheater had been taken out, so absence of header allowed the chimney to be fitted on the centre line of the smokebox. As this smokebox was retained by the tank engine, the chimney on No.6077 (9930) was further back than any of the other twelve.

(below) Nos.69928 and 69929 were at Langwith Junction shed until June 1958 and as the water there was very hard, a small vertical pipe was put on top of the left hand tank, near the front, so that water treatment tablets could be fed into the perforated pipe inside the tank. No.69928 had this fitting from January 1953.

5044 cont./
22983 9/4/55.

SHEDS:
Retford.
Langwith Jct. 13/2/44.
Mexborough 6/5/44.
Selby 17/9/44.
Gateshead 13/12/44.
Selby 6/2/49.

RENUMBERED:
9931 30/6/46.
69931 27/1/49.

CONDEMNED: 26/11/58.
Cut up at Gorton.

5959

Doncaster, rebuilt from Q4.

To traffic 4/3/1944.

REPAIRS:
Gor. 17/5—21/6/47.**G.**
Gor. 8/11—3/12/49.**G.**
Gor. 20/7—16/8/52.**G.**
Gor. 19—21/8/52.**N/C.**
Gor. 2/3—16/4/55.**G.**
Gor. 25—26/4/55.**N/C.**
Gor. 1/10—3/11/56.**C/L.**
Gor. 6—7/11/56.**N/C.**

BOILERS:
3745.
3765 21/6/47.
3755 3/12/49.
22989 21/8/52.
22988 16/4/55.

SHEDS:
Ardsley.
Mexborough 14/4/44.
Darnall 2/7/44.
Mexborough 17/8/44.
Doncaster 25/8/46.
Frodingham 24/9/46.

RENUMBERED:
9932 7/4/46.
69932 3/12/49.

CONDEMNED: 12/11/58.
Into Gor. for cut up 15/11/58.

5087

Doncaster, rebuilt from Q4.

To traffic 20/5/1944.

REPAIRS:
Dar. 14/8—19/9/46.**L.**
Side tank fractured.
Dar. 26/4—11/6/48.**G.**
Dar. 15/12/48—14/1/49.**C/L.**
Left hand tank fractured.
Gor. 13/11/51—11/1/52.**G.**
Gor. 5/7—2/9/55.**G.**
Gor. 30/9—26/10/57.**C/L.**
Gor. 19/8—20/9/58.**C/L.**
Gor. 4/12/58. *Not repaired.*

BOILERS:
643.
22987 11/1/52.
22994 2/9/55.

SHEDS:
Barnsley.
Ardsley 26/6/44.
Mexborough 19/7/44.
Dairycoates 17/9/44.
Gateshead 13/12/44.
Selby 6/2/49.

RENUMBERED:
9933 30/6/46.
69933 11/6/48.

CONDEMNED: 11/12/58.
Cut up at Gorton.

5068

Doncaster, rebuilt from Q4.

To traffic 6/9/1944.

REPAIRS:
Gor. 8/5—12/6/48.**G.**
Gor. 14/2—31/3/51.**G.**
Gor. 12/11—19/12/53.**G.**
Gor. 22—31/12/53.**N/C.**
Gor. 24/6—29/9/56.**G.**
Gor. 1—17/10/56.**N/C.**

BOILERS:
3750.
3766 12/6/48.
22982 31/3/51.
22981 19/12/53.
22986 29/9/56.

SHEDS:
Barnsley.
Mexborough 6/10/44.
Doncaster 25/8/46.
Frodingham 26/9/46.

RENUMBERED:
9934 7/4/46.
69934 12/6/48.

CONDEMNED: 20/8/59.
Into Dar. for cut up 22/8/59.

5147

Doncaster, rebuilt from Q4.

To traffic 16/1/1945.

REPAIRS:
Gor. 28/8—18/9/48.**G.**
Gor. 5/6—11/8/51.**G.**
Gor. 14/2—20/3/54.**G.**
Gor. 23/3—2/4/54.**N/C.**
Gor. 5/7—31/8/57.**G.**
Gor. 3—14/9/57.**N/C.**

BOILERS:
3755.
3753 18/9/48.
22985 11/8/51.
22984 20/3/54.
22982 31/8/57.

SHEDS:
Mexborough.
Doncaster 25/8/46.
Frodingham 26/9/46.

RENUMBERED:
9935 27/1/46.
69935 18/9/48.

CONDEMNED: 3/9/59.
Into Dar. for cut up 26/9/59.

6179

Doncaster, rebuilt from Q4.

To traffic 28/4/1945.

REPAIRS:
Gor. 24/7—28/8/48.**G.**
Gor. 29/5—30/6/51.**G.**
Gor. 24/1—6/3/54.**G.**
New cylinders.
Gor. 9—31/3/54.**N/C.**
Gor. 12/9—10/11/56.**G.**
Gor. 13—17/11/56.**N/C.**

Gor. 8—26/4/58.**C/L.**

BOILERS:
3746.
3750 28/8/48.
22983 30/6/51.
22982 6/3/54.
22987 10/11/56.

SHEDS:
Mexborough.
Doncaster 25/8/46.
Frodingham 28/9/46.

RENUMBERED:
9936 26/5/46.
69936 28/8/48.
CONDEMNED: 15/9/59.
Into Dar. for cut up 26/9/59.

5138

Doncaster, rebuilt from Q4.

To traffic 8/9/1945.

REPAIRS:
Gor. 3/7—21/8/48.**G.**
Gor. 2—30/6/51.**G.**
New cylinders.
Gor. 23/1—13/2/54.**G.**

BOILERS:
3753.
3745 21/8/48.
22984 30/6/51.
22992 13/2/54.

SHEDS:
Ardsley.
Mexborough 19/9/45.
Doncaster 25/8/46.
Frodingham 28/9/46.
RENUMBERED:
9937 7/4/46.
69937 21/8/48.

CONDEMNED: 5/11/56.
Into Gor. for cut up 10/11/56.

WORKS CODES:- Cw - Cowlairs. Dar- Darlington. Don - Doncaster. Ghd - Gateshead. Gor - Gorton. Inv - Inverurie. Str - Stratford.
REPAIR CODES:- **C/H** - Casual Heavy. **C/L** - Casual Light. **G** - General. **H** - Heavy. **H/I** - Heavy Intermediate. **L** - Light. **L/I** - Light Intermediate. **N/C** - Non-Classified.

85

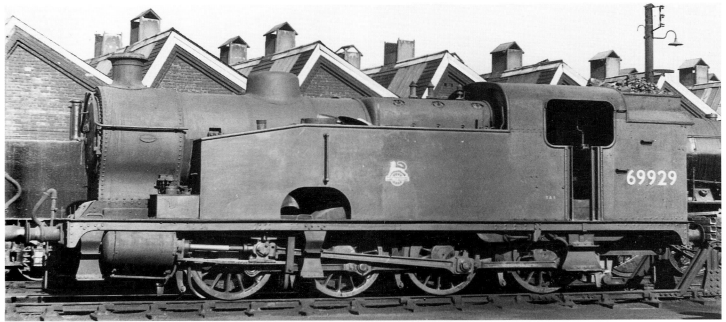

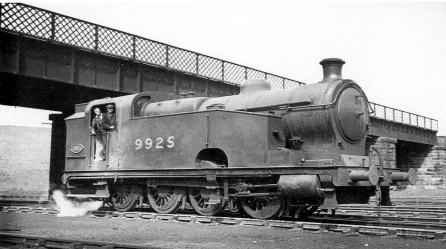

No.69929's water treatment pipe, put on in October 1955, was noticeably shorter, but served equally well. Only these two were so fitted.

In the conversion it was possible to retain the original front buffer beam, and all except two also kept GC type buffers. Those two were 6139 (9927) and 5147 (9935) which were given Group Standard buffers, with square base and stepped casing.

Ex Cowlairs on 3rd March 1951 No.69925 had been changed to Group Standard buffers, the only one so altered.

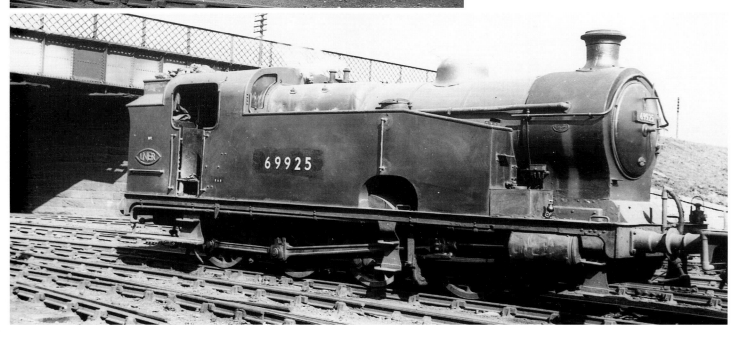

On 26th August 1943 Nos.5058 (9925) and 6139 (9927) were sent to Eastfield and then worked from that shed to withdrawal. As was customary on NBR shunting engines they were soon fitted with a riding step and an extra rail across the bunker.

Step and rail for the shunter was fitted on both sides of the engine. Although No.9927 had GS buffers and hook, it kept the 3-link loose coupling and served entirely as a goods shunter.

(below) In 1948, No.69925 was tried on banking passenger trains up Cowlairs incline out of Glasgow (Queen Street) station. For this work its three-link coupling was changed to a screw-adjustable type, and a bracket was fitted on the smokebox to carry the guide wheel for an operating wire to a slip-coupling. The trial was brief, and the slip-coupling equipment soon discarded, but the screw coupling was kept to August 1954 withdrawal.

No.69927 was an oddity in retaining its upper lamp iron in the original position and never having it moved on to the smokebox door.

Normal buffer heads were circular, and No.9932 had that type to November 1949 (*see* photo 32 page XX). When ex works 3rd December 1949 it had been fitted with GCR type oval heads and was also changed to screw coupling.

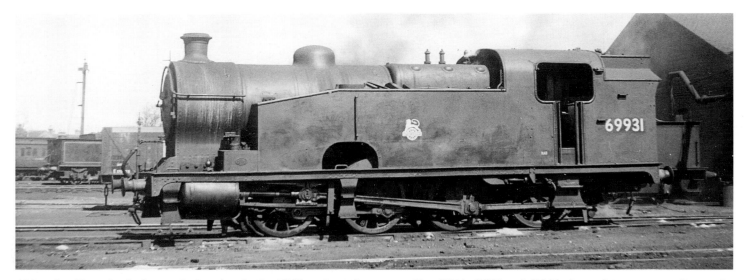

Although still used only for goods shunting, in the 1950's at least three more, Nos.69931, 69934 and 69946, changed to screw coupling at the front.

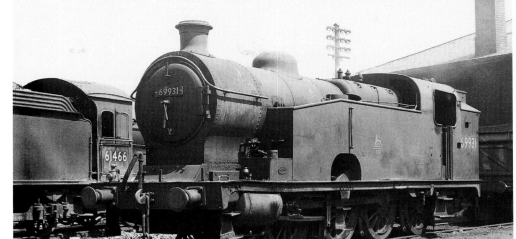

Ex works 9th April 1955, No.69931 had reverted to 3-link loose coupling which it still had at November 1958 withdrawal.

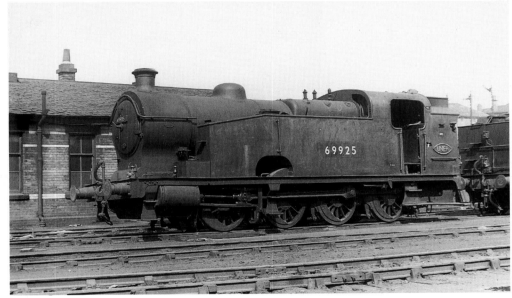

No.69925 only got that BR number on 3rd March 1951 ex a heavy/intermediate repair at which Cowlairs did not repaint it. That accounts for it keeping small figures, and still on the tank. Withdrawn 13th August 1954, at its next works visit, it kept the style shown, so never carried BR lettering or the emblem.

Between 27th January and 24th November 1946 all were renumbered to 9925 to 9937 in order of date they became Q1 class. No.5138 changed to 9937 on Sunday 7th April 1946 at Mexborough shed and the paint used for the 6in. stencil figures was clearly not waterproof.

The first conversion introduced a different livery style. Just at that point, the LNER was being cut to NE, but on Q1 class only the number was put on by transfers, A cast plate of the LNER totem was put on the bunker to show ownership. The background was light blue with white letters and all thirteen got this style. Engine painting was, and remained, unlined black.

This heavy shunting tank was included in Thompson's proposed Standard Classes, so on 27th January 1944 newly converted No.5044 was used to provide this illustration for the Memo. to the Locomotive Committee (*see* also page 80). Note NE instead of a cast plate for the portrait.

When renumbering was implemented in 1946 the nine at Southern Area sheds got their new numbers in only 6in. stencils. The two in Scottish Area, Nos.9925 and 9927 (*see* page 82) and the two in North Eastern Area, Nos.9931 and 9933 (*see* page 84) were dealt with by normal 12in. shaded transfers.

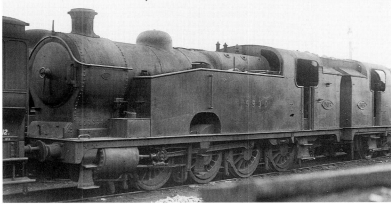

No.9930 done at Mexborough 26th May 1946 had the stencil figures finished off properly. No.9935 done there as early as 27th January 1946 showed that it had been done by stencilling (*see* previous illustration).

No.9932 entered Gorton for general repair on 17th May 1947 and before being returned to traffic was painted green with black edging and white lining for this official photograph. When ex works 21st June 1947 it had been repainted unlined black.

Ex Cowlairs 15th July 1948 from general repair, No.69927 had number moved to the bunker where it was put above the totem plate. This high position led to the matching tank lettering being above centre and having an odd appearance (*see* also page 88). The two Scottish engines kept the LNER totem until they were withdrawn.

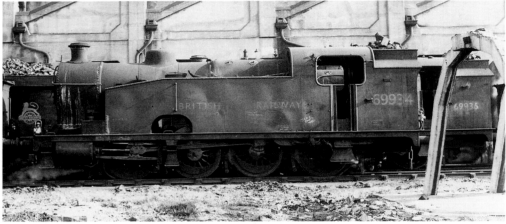

No.69934, ex Gorton 12th June 1948 was the only one to get 6in. BRITISH RAILWAYS and 12in. numbers. The latter was moved from tank to bunker from which the LNER totem had been discarded. Note painted, unshaded numbers had the LNER modification to the Gill sans numbers 6 and 9.

The two NE Area engines only went on Gorton maintenance from January 1952. No.69933 was ex Darlington 11th June 1948 with matching figures and letters but with modified 6 and 9. The totem plate was removed but no smokebox number plate had been fitted. No.69931 got BR numbering at a Gateshead light repair 27th January 1949, and then went straight to emblem ex Darlington 7th October 1950.

Between 21st August and 2nd October, 1948, Gorton put five into this BR style using correct Gill sans 6 and 9 on the bunker but the modified variety on the smokebox number plate. These were Nos.69937 (21/8), 69936 (28/8), 69926 (11/9), 69935 (18/9) and 69929 (2/10). The other three, 69928 (20/8/49), 69930 (19/11/49) and 69932 (3/12/49), also got BRITISH RAILWAYS and had correct 6 and 9 on smokebox plate (*see* page 88).

No.69931 ex Darlington on 7th October 1950 was the first to change to the BR emblem with 69928 on 16th December 1950 the first from Gorton. Apart from 69925 this painting style was then carried by all the others until withdrawal.

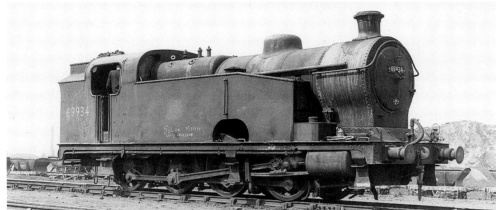

Although the BR crest was used by some classes from its April 1957 introduction, only 69935 (31/8/57) and 69928 (12/10/57) had a general repair after that date but neither got the crest. When No.69936 was withdrawn on 15th September 1959 Class Q1 was extinct.

69928 from 20th August 1949 had been 9928 from 7th April 1946 and 5048 when it became Q1 on 20th March 1943. On 13th April 1943 it left Barnsley for Langwith Jct., went to Immingham 28th August 1944 but returned to Langwith 1st October. Working from there on 20th August 1951 it was on this coal train at Warsop. On 15th June 1958 it moved to Frodingham from where it was withdrawn 20th August 1959.

Another Langwith Junction engine, No.69929, waits for a signal at Shirebrook North on 20th June 1952. With 69928 it moved to Frodingham in 1958 and was also withdrawn in August 1959 but a week after 69928.

(below) No.69931 left Gateshead 6th February 1949 and moved to Selby to start work at the gravity yard at Gascoigne Wood where it was caught on film shortly before withdrawal.